Money is a Way of Life

Money is a Way of Life

ANNA MOTSON

London

MICHAEL JOSEPH

First published in Great Britain by Michael Joseph Ltd
52 Bedford Square, London WC1B 3EF
1974

ISBN 0 7181 1122 2

Set and printed in Great Britain
by Northumberland Press Limited, Gateshead
in Baskerville eleven on fourteen point,
on paper supplied by P. F. Bingham Ltd,
and bound by Dorstel Press, Harlow

Contents

Introduction

Money is essentially absurd. It makes us feel embarrassed when we have too little and even more embarrassed when we have too much. We feel good when we give it away and still better when we get something for nothing. And while we are as sensitive about our income as we are about our age, we take a voyeur's pleasure in probing the incomes of others.

While this element of the absurd is by no means peculiar to the age in which we live, it is undoubtedly becoming more noticeable. Men who make money make headlines, and those who had once never heard of the balance of payments now accept it as front page news. Time that is not spent making money is largely spent talking about it, and the increasing preoccupation with financial security and investment is matched by the growing popularity of pursuits such as bingo and gambling. The game of Monopoly has become a classic in its field, and the national newspaper with the least worries about its future is the blushing *Financial Times*. There is no doubt about it: money matters, and the more familiar we are with it the more it seems to fascinate.

Clearly much of the fascination of money stems from the fact that we cannot do without it, and are constantly being lured by the growing number of marvellous things we can do with it. Glossy brochures tempt the eye with romantic cut-price holidays in faraway lands; rosy advertisements weaken the will with their visions of paradise personified—a new car, a better washing machine, a bigger house. Also, of course, in the credit-happy seventies, you do not even have to have money in order to spend it. The old English saying, 'Samson was a strong man, but he could not pay money before he had it', is no longer true. What is true is that we are becoming so pressurized, so mesmerized by money that it threatens to take over as an end in itself rather than a means to an end. We are forgetting what money is for, like the lecherous 80-year-old man who still runs after girls but is unable to remember why.

It was not always so, and perhaps the fact that it is so now is no more than the inevitable result of economic progress. In primitive times goods were exchanged for goods, and there was no such thing as speculation or credit. The introduction of money changed all that by altering the whole concept of wealth. Here was a commodity, tangible, visible, and portable too, that could easily be exchanged for anything. In due course it became capable of buying not only material things but abstracts such as services and time, while for those in positions of authority it provided the means of satisfying their own particular ambitions, both good and bad.

With the passing of time, money has evolved into a highly sophisticated and complex commodity. It now buys more things for a wider range of people than ever before, from status and social mobility to personal pleasure, security, protection and comfort. It can be invested in stocks and shares, land, art or precious stones, or used to buy affection, freedom and friendship. It can bring enormous advantages and it can do positive harm, for from being simply a means of exchange money has developed into a powerful lever in its own right.

Yet there are weaknesses in this vastly complicated financial structure, the main one being that the value of money is far from constant. A sound investment today could well become a total loss tomorrow, while money put by for the future will soon be worth a fraction of its original buying power unless adequate precautions are taken to protect it. Even then there is always the danger of theft or devaluation, so that those who have money find that they worry just as much as those who have none.

The result is that only those who are above money, such as the religious and the idealistic, can be said to be truly free. For those of us who are in any way concerned with the process of money-making are bound to be subject to fears of not getting enough or of losing what we have. Moreover we have become prey to wrapping up our money in whatever it can buy, a tendency that is both created and encouraged by advertising. Possessions and money have therefore become our only means of safety and security and hence (since money is elusive and transitory) the cause of our insecurity.

There is abundant evidence to show that we have allowed money to achieve a position of supreme importance in our lives. But, as in the case of other things of similar importance such as sex and religion, we are ashamed to admit just how much it matters to us. So we lie about it. These lies are not simply confined to particular instances in our daily lives: we are brought up on them and they form part of our heritage. Sayings handed down from generation to generation indicate something of the confusion and hypocrisy of our attitude towards money.

First of all we pass on to our children a moral code of behaviour that is quite contrary to the practice of everyday life, and we then urge them to break it and even rebuke them if they fail to do so. We tell them, for instance, that the love of money is the root of all evil and then encourage them to flirt with the rich and follow a career that promises high rewards and early retirement. We tell them that necessity is the mother of invention, and then go to great lengths to set up trusts and provide insurance for their future so that they will never be in need. We tell them that the best things in life are free, but we don't really believe it and neither do they.

It is, of course, partly habit that makes us go on saying these things, but it is an indication, too, of our reluctance to admit to ourselves just how powerful money has become. It is a reluctance that quickly turns into defensiveness whenever the conversation strays into the forbidden territory of personal finance, for money is the last of the taboo subjects. It is quite permissible to talk about matters of economics and high finance, but people recoil with horror when asked the simple question, 'How much do you earn?' This unwillingness to discuss their financial affairs seems astonishing in view of the fact that most people spend the greater part of their lives working at something they do not really enjoy, simply in order to pay their way. Money dominates our existence to a frightening extent, and for this reason alone it should be talked about.

That is the purpose, and also the subject matter, of this book. In it people from all walks of life discuss their own personal feelings and attitudes towards money: how they make it, why they want it, what it does to them and what they will do for it. Each individual speaks only for himself, giving us an insight into his own particular lifestyle, and, taken together, these personal opinions add up to a fascinating social kaleidoscope of our times.

The starting point of the book is the necessity of earning an adequate income. This drives most people into regular jobs with regular hours and before long work (often dull and unrewarding in itself) becomes the most important factor in day to day living. Far from frowning upon this state of affairs, society develops it one stage further by encouraging people to live above their means. Advertising creates desires and needs that consumers never knew they had, and credit facilities are readily available to provide the means of satisfying them. Before long the individual becomes enmeshed in a network of credit cards, hire purchase agreements, loans, overdrafts, mortgages and insurance schemes which effectively guarantee that he will spend the rest of his working life paying off his creditors.

The best way to avoid being a permanent debtor is of course to make or win enough money to escape from the pressures of financial necessity. Making it is easy for some, impossible for others, and while most people wait and hope that luck will bring them a fortune on the football pools, other more desperate individuals turn to crime. In each case the way that a person comes by his money leaves an indelible mark not only on his appearance but also on his character, personality and general outlook. This is particularly evident in all the people who have contributed to the first part of this book, from the self-made millionaire and the gas fitter to the prostitute and the thief. In each case the need for money and the desire for money have made them what they are.

For some individuals, however, money is unimportant in itself. It matters only because it is a means to a particular end for which they crave. To the junkie money means drugs, to the compulsive gambler it means the ability to go on betting. And whether the junkie dies is as irrelevant to him as losing is to the gambler.

The happiest people in the book are those who have been able to come to terms with money and put it in its proper perspective. The priest, the nun and the hippy living in a commune are all driven by something stronger than material values. And while their life-style cannot be expected to appeal to more than a small minority, their inner peace of mind must be enviable to many.

In writing this book it seemed to me that everyone can learn something from the people who have contributed to it. There is no moral, no lesson to be learnt—there cannot be—only, perhaps, that no-one can be truly free within a materialistic capitalist society.

Part One

MAKING MONEY

CHAPTER ONE

The daily grind

Every morning for the past 41 years George Thompson has put on a pair of baggy overalls and cycled to the South Eastern Gas Board to begin his day's work as a gas fitter. Last year he was presented with a gold watch, but his weekly wage is still only £24, and when he retires in about ten years' time (he is now 54 years old) he will receive a pension of about £1.50 a week.

George is a proud man of solid working-class stock. Tall and heavily built, with a slow smile, his large, capable hands are permanently darkened by years of ingrained dirt. His 80-year-old father Charles was a gas fitter before him in the days when lamp-lighters were a familiar sight, and his 25-year-old son John has gone into the industry too. The Thompsons—Charles, George, wife Hazelle and four children—live together in a small, semi-detached house in Kingston, Surrey, and they are a close family. Between them they do everything that needs doing around the house, painting, decorating, rewiring, wallpapering, and at one time George even used to mend the family's shoes. Things are better now, and there is no longer any real hardship. In fact George feels strongly that the youngsters of today do not really know what hardship is.

'I left school at 13, and started work the next day as an apprentice gas fitter earning fourteen shillings a week. I used to hand it all over to my parents, who gave me back two shillings a week as pocket money. That was enough to buy tea and buns through the week in those days. I never resented it, never gave it a second thought, because that's how things were then. One was lucky to have a job at all.'

That was the pattern of George Thompson's life until the outbreak of war in 1939 when, at the age of 20, he joined the army. His weekly take-home pay was then nineteen shillings, a rise of just a shilling a year. The army was little more than an interlude—it did not reshape his view of the world or make him want bigger and better things. The most important event as far as he was concerned was meeting Hazelle, a plump Norfolk girl in the land army, who became his wife as soon as the war was over. In 1946 George went back to life in the gas industry.

'We rented a couple of rooms for £4 a week to begin with, but when John arrived things became a bit more difficult and we had to live apart for a while. Screaming babies aren't too popular with landlords. But then we managed to rent a house—it was quite near here actually—and stayed there for close on 20 years. All the kids, John, David, Philip and Margaret, could run riot there without bothering anyone, and when we were offered the chance of buying it for £1,000 of course we jumped at it. We thought that was the ultimate, having a home of our own, but we didn't know just how lucky we were because last January the area was scheduled for redevelopment and the property people offered us £22,000 to move out. We just couldn't believe it—it was like winning the pools.

'We bought this house straight out for £16,500. I've never owed money for anything and I hated the idea of a mortgage. Then, for the first time in my life, I opened a bank account to invest what was left of the money. I can honestly say I've got everything I've always dreamed about now—a house of my own and a couple of thousand in the bank. That's all I need.

'Of course it wasn't easy bringing up a family on the kind of salary I get, but I absolutely refused to let my wife go out to work. The way I look at it is that if I can't look after them on the money I earn then I'm not much good to them. Both Hazelle and I would much rather go without things than have her go out to work.

'Neither of us cares very much for material things anyway. We don't hanker after money, and, like I said, we never buy anything on credit. As long as we have enough to take care of immediate needs, that's all that matters. Not that I don't believe I'm *worth* more—I think the responsibility of the job and the experience of 40 years in the industry makes me worth a hell of a lot more—but money for money's sake doesn't interest me at all. All these people who agitate for more pay and less working hours don't know what they're at. Who's going to pay the wages if there's no productivity?

'I can honestly say there isn't anyone in the world I'm jealous of, or anything I secretly hanker after. God knows I see enough of these moneyed people every day. I do the stockbroker belt regularly and I know them all, the smooth talkers with their Rolls Royces and their heated indoor swimming pools. There isn't one of them I envy. Why? Because very few of them are happy, that's why. Their money keeps them awake at night. They feel more insecure having everything than I do having nothing. They're afraid of losing what they've got. If I have nothing I can work, I have my hands, but what have they got? Money is evil. I don't want it. It does strange things to you.

'Lots of these people, you can tell they're not happy by their homes. They don't look lived in, or loved in, if you know what I mean. When I go round to fix something, as soon as I make the slightest mess on the floor someone rushes up with a dustpan and brush to sweep it up. You feel you're intruding, it's not like being in a home at all.

'I've never resented working. I've always believed, and I still believe, that we're put on this earth to do some good for the community. And I've done that. To me, that's what life is about, not lazing around on a yacht in the Mediterranean somewhere. I know I don't get thanked for it and when I retire I shall get about £1.50 a week pension, that's all. But if I had my life over again, I wouldn't change it.

'I wouldn't stop working even if I won the pools. I'd invest the money and forget about it. I wouldn't know what to do with myself if I didn't work. It's the whole environment I enjoy, getting out, meeting people, feeling I've done something at the end of the day. If you stopped working, your brain would go mouldy.

'I must say Hazelle's been marvellous. She's a wonderful manager and never complains—I'm sure we would never have got by if it hadn't been for her. Even when we hardly had two pennies to rub together, she still managed to get a warm meal together somehow. Our kids always had full tummies when they went to bed at night. In fact I think we must have made them too comfortable because none of them want to leave!

'Kids nowadays have a completely different attitude towards money. They want everything *now,* they're not content to climb up the ladder like we were. Apprentices today start at about two-thirds of what I get, it's the only way they can keep people coming into the industry, but it's not right all the same. They don't know anything, so how can they be worth that much?

'But then I know material things mean a lot more to the

youngsters today. My son would be quite lost without his car, for instance, whereas I've never had a car and I don't want one, neither does the wife. I've always had a bicycle until a little while ago when I bought a motorcycle. Hazette and I are always saying that the real trouble with young people is that they don't know what it's like to go without. Everyone ought to experience that.'

Hazelle, who has just appeared in the doorway, nods in agreement. She is small, round and smiling—clearly a woman who enjoys the homely arts of cooking, baking and mothering—and her unmade-up face is framed by short, tightly curled grey hair. She brushes the flour from her hands and settles herself at one end of the patterned sofa, glancing quickly at the clock to see how long she can stay away from the kitchen.

'Of course it wasn't easy bringing up a family of four on 46 shillings a week,' she says, 'but I suppose it was made easier by the fact that George and I have always been very happy together. We haven't had half a dozen quarrels in over 25 years, and whatever the problem was, we always faced it together.

'Not being one to fuss much over myself, I never felt hard done by because we were short of money. Now I go to the hairdresser about once a fortnight, just to have my hair curled, but I don't bother much with dressing-up. If I see something special then George gives me the money to buy it. I wear make-up occasionally if we go out somewhere special, a dinner dance or something like that, but I've never been one to pretty myself with nail polish and so on. If God had wanted women to have coloured nails he'd have made them that way. Needless to say my daughter Margaret doesn't agree with me. She's 15 and seems to spend all her time painting her nails in all kinds of outlandish colours.

'They're good kids, though, all of them. I think that not having quite so much money has probably made us closer as a family. Of course we have our ups and downs, that's only natural, but the kids never thought of leaving when they started work, and life still revolves very much round the home. I don't think it would have been the same if we'd been rich somehow.

'We always go on holiday together, even now. Usually it's to somewhere in England, not because we don't want to go abroad but I suppose we couldn't afford it for such a long time that now it's just become a habit. Still, we've made up our minds to be a bit more adventurous now that we've got the money to do it with, take advantage of a few of those package holidays in Spain and places. John brought some brochures just the other day in fact. He says we'll have to decide soon where we want to go next year, else we'll end up in Blackpool or Southend again.'

Retirement is a prospect which frightens neither George nor Hazelle. They have a quarter-acre allotment near their home where George—a keen gardener—spends most of his free time. At the moment he produces a ton of potatoes a year, and enough vegetables and fruit to reduce the family's food bill considerably. When he gives up work he hopes to expand his activities in this direction, perhaps producing enough to be able to sell to the public and provide Hazelle and himself with a small income.

'Just as long as I have a roof over my head, I'm really not bothered,' he says cheerfully. 'I've had a good life, a useful life I hope, and that's what it's all about, not making money. Personally I think that what I've done is much more difficult and much more satisfying than getting rich. I've kept a wife, brought up four kids and managed to buy my own home as well—and on a salary of £24 a week I'd say that's quite an achievement.'

George Thompson's attitude seems to reflect the feelings of only a minority of the working population. Most people dream of escaping from the strictures of daily life, the routines and often the boredom of their waking hours. If they did not have to worry about mortgages, rents, rates, school fees, monthly bills, it is doubtful if most of them would continue working.

There is only one way to escape the tyranny of a nine-to-five existence and all that goes with it, and that is to make enough money to do as you please. Just how much this would amount to is impossible to say, for it varies from individual to individual and from year to year, but certainly most people are far from achieving financial freedom. The vast majority of adult citizens are employees owning little more than their household goods and the clothes on their backs. Most are not even as lucky as George Thompson, and have mortgaged homes in which the furniture is either second-hand or bought on hire purchase, together with the family car. The trappings of affluence bought on credit are not at all the same thing as the possession of wealth. A self-made millionaire and a football pools winner give us a glimpse of what it is like to be really rich.

CHAPTER TWO

Riches

The fact that most people can barely manage to meet their financial commitments every month goes a long way towards explaining the aura of glamour that hangs over the lives of the rich like a permanent heat haze. The activities of multi-millionaires Howard Hughes, Paul Getty and Aristotle Onassis are automatically front page news, for wealth on a scale such as this is quite beyond the comprehension of most people.

The gulf is widened still further by the fact that, in spite of the abundance of help and advice regularly offered in newspapers and magazines on how to make money, there is no secret formula. Those who are not born rich must either marry someone rich or break away and make it on their own. The alternative is to fill in a football pools coupon every week and hope for a miracle. Whichever way you look at it, making money is not easy and few people succeed in reaching the millionaire class. The two people who have contributed to this chapter are part of the small minority who have achieved their ambition and who now consider themselves to be wealthy. Wealth is in fact the only thing that they do have in common, for as individuals they could not be further apart. Each of them came by his money in a different way—Jack Sinclair, businessman, is a self-made millionaire, while Joe Donald, bricklayer, woke up one morning to find that Vernons pools had at last made his wildest dreams come true.

Jack Sinclair, at 53, is the younger of the two. He is chairman and managing director of a car business he created twenty years ago and which has now become one of the largest and most successful operations of its kind in the world. His main concern is auctions, and the turnover from his company's many centres all over the country is now running at more than £1 million a week, with plans for expansion both at home and in Europe. Jack Sinclair has other financial interests as well—property, holiday camps, pubs and clubs among them—and he estimates his own personal fortune at well over £6 million.

Money clearly suits him. A deliberate dresser with only a touch of grey in his reddish blond head of hair, he looks younger than his years, and the only direct evidence of good living is the gently rounded paunch curving from his well-built frame. He unashamedly enjoys the flamboyance that money allows: he drinks champagne constantly, has a new Rolls Royce every year, a permanent fleet of servants, and lives with his fifth wife in a large country house which boasts, among other things, a private golf course and a stable of racehorses. It goes without saying that he drives a car with his initials on the number plate and flies a private plane.

His fifth wife is younger now than his first wife was when he married her thirty-six years ago, and his five children (by three different mothers) range in age from 22 to one year. To Jack Sinclair money means that he can do what he wants to do when he wants to do it, and the excitement never palls. A forthright man with bright eyes and a merry laugh, his language is frequently vulgar and a liberal sprinkling of four-letter words is taken for granted, no matter in whose company he might find himself. He has all the confidence in the world, the confidence that comes from knowing that, as far as making money is concerned, he has come out on top.

'Money, darling, is simply a game—it's like Monopoly only for real. The reason I make money is because I'm cleverer than everyone else, I always was. Why do you think they made me the youngest lieutenant in the navy during the war? Because I was bright, that's why, and because I refused to accept other people's bullshit. Most people haven't got the guts to stand up and say no, but me, I don't give a monkey's fart for that kind of thing.

'I came out of the navy with £600 in my pocket, not exactly rich but not poor either. My family were the sort of people who were rolling in money one day and bankrupt the next, so I was used to both. I'm grateful for that, bloody grateful, because it taught me not to give a hang for security. You never make a penny without taking risks and most people are too shit-scared to do it, aren't they? They're all so insecure, they worry about losing their pension or ending up without a roof over their head or some other crap like that. When you know what it's like to have nothing you don't worry about it. I lost everything eight years ago—I had debts of £½ million—but I didn't care. I just went ahead and made some more. How did I do it? With paper, darling, that's how.

'I started the car business almost by accident really. After the war when I came out of the navy I bought a couple of cars very cheaply, and I thought I'd try and sell them. You could rent a field for £1 a day then, so the best way of doing it was obviously to pitch a tent and try and auction them off. I didn't expect much response to be quite honest, but when the great day came bugger me if forty people didn't turn up! I sold those cars for about twice the amount I paid for them and all it cost me was a quid. So I thought to myself, there's money in this game Jack, and from then on I never looked back.

'Is money important to me? It's important to everyone, darling, of course it is. Those who say it isn't are the ones who can't make it or don't have it. Either that or they're lying. I enjoy my money, that's what it's for, isn't it? I live the way I want to live and I do the things I want to do. I have a lovely house, my children are well provided for, I'm married to a super bird. That's what life's about, not sweating it out in some stuffy office waiting to retire. No, I don't think it's a bad thing for my kids to know they'll never starve—life is quite enough of a challenge as it is without having to worry about making money as well.

'I suppose, looking back, that at least one of my previous marriages broke up because I was away from home too much, too concerned with making money and building up the business. I don't regret it, not now, but I know she does. I look after her though, she has a house in the country and staff to take care of her. I didn't have to do that, you know, she ran off with someone else and it was me that divorced her in the end. But she never married again, says she never wants to, in fact she's fucking sorry she ever left me. It was my fault really though, that's why I look after her. I like women, I spend a lot of money on them and they give me a lot of pleasure in return. There's nothing wrong with that, is there? The occasional screw isn't going to bust up my marriage, and in any case life is far too short to worry about moral crap like that.

'Yes, I suppose I am very possessive about what I've got—wouldn't you be? I've never been burgled, for the simple reason that when I caught someone trying to break into my house a few years ago I shot at him. I didn't hit him but he was caught and there was a hell of a fuss about it in the papers. When the case came up in court the judge asked me what right I thought I had to shoot at someone like that, so I told him I had exactly the same right as that bastard had to enter my premises. I didn't fight in the fucking war for nothing. No-one tells me what to do on my property, and I told the judge that if it ever happened again I'd do just the same thing—and I would too, only next time I'd make sure not to miss. I've always had dogs since then, three of them sleeping in outside kennels. That kind of thing soon gets round in the underworld, you know; they know by now that if the dogs don't get them I'll bloody well shoot them.

'No, I don't worry about people trying to get to know me for my money and I don't give a shit if my friends are rich or poor either. Of course there's always bound to be some wise guy somewhere waiting to turn you over but so what? You just have to keep your wits about you, that's all. Hangers-on soon learn that I give when I want and to whom I choose. If I don't choose then I don't give.

'I don't see any way at all in which my business can possibly go bankrupt, there isn't a loophole in it anywhere. The secret of success, darling, is to stick to what you know, nothing else. I know the car business inside out and I know everyone who works for me personally. They're well looked after, my people; I pay them well, they all get BUPA coverage on the firm and free holidays in Europe when they've been with me for ten years or more. I've never had a strike here, not once, nor even a threat of one. They know when they're well off, my men.

'I did try to start a new line in engineering a few years ago, but it was a disastrous mistake. That's why I say stick to what you damn well know. I woke up one morning and decided to close it down, write it off, just like that. I gave everyone the sack and it was over, finished. Well, either they went bankrupt or else I did and I was sure as hell it wasn't going to be me.

'I have no sympathy for the unemployed anyway—most of them don't want to work in any case. Look at the north of England. It's fashionable to be unemployed up there and it's bloody easy to live off the state, so why not? If anyone does have a job, all the others lean out of the window in their dressing gowns and jeer at him as he goes off to work in the morning, I've seen them. By the end of the week no-one on the estate's working any more.

'Has money changed me? No, not a bit. I still do the same things I did before, the only difference is that I can afford to do them now whereas before I couldn't. People who think rich will always live rich, no matter how poor they are, just as those who think poor will never really know what it's like to be anything else. It's just an attitude of mind really, isn't it?'

Joe and Betty Donald would probably agree with that. Two years ago they were living in a £500 terraced house on the outskirts of London. Every morning, Joe, a small, tough man with greying hair, would pick up his overalls and set off for the building site, while Betty, with no children to look after, went off to her job in an insurance office. In the evening they would go down to the pub for a drink and a chat with their friends; occasionally they went out for a meal. It was the kind of life thousands of people lead, in fact because they had no children to clothe and feed the Donalds would have been better off than most of their friends if they had not undertaken to look after Betty's ageing mother and stepfather. As it was, the £40 a week they earned between them did not go very far, and after meeting the basic costs of day to day living there was little left for luxuries. What worried the Donalds, however, was not the lack of luxury but the prospect of their own retirement. Sometimes they would joke about it with their friends down at the pub. 'Don't worry, we'll win the pools before then! ' Joe used to say with a grin.

And that is exactly what happened. Early one morning in July 1971, two men in dark suits knocked on the front door of the small, terraced house. They had come, they said, to congratulate Mr and Mrs Joe Donald on a first dividend Vernons pools win of close on £100,000. Suddenly Joe and Betty Donald were rich.

It took them a little while to realize what that meant. For a month they carried on as before, both working at their regular jobs while the cheque remained in the bank, untouched. Then, when he felt he had become used to the idea, Joe gave in his notice, bought a Rover 2000 and booked a first-class cabin on a six-months' luxury cruise. Betty gave up her job as well, bought six long evening dresses in the summer sales in anticipation of their trip, and began looking for a new house in a new district. A few days before the ship sailed they found what they were looking for, a beautiful but dilapidated four-hundred-year-old farmhouse, miles from anywhere in the Norfolk countryside. They bought it for £15,000 and left instructions with the builders who were to complete the work while they were away.

Needless to say, it took very much longer than they had expected and when they returned from their first taste of luxury living their dream house was far from ready. Unperturbed, Joe and Betty moved in together with Madge, one of Betty's cousins from London, and while the builders were laying down floors and putting in doors they busied themselves hanging wallpaper and choosing curtains. Even now, more than two years later, there are still things to be done but to all intents and purposes the transformation is complete. The six bedrooms are furnished and carpeted, the beds made up ready for guests; a log fire burns merrily in the long, oak-beamed living room downstairs, and in the grounds behind the farmhouse there are two small ponds guarded by ornamental gnomes, storks and cherubs. The rest of the two acres of land is still wild but there is plenty of time to decide what to do with that—perhaps they will even sell some of it. Joe is certainly not worried about it; in fact as he settles back into one of the new gold and chintz armchairs, cigar in hand, contentedly watching Betty, plump in a pink crimplene trouser suit, busying herself in the kitchen, it seems evident that there is little these days that worries either of them.

'I think,' Joe says carefully, 'that more than anything this money means security for both of us. It's a wonderful thing to know that you no longer have to worry about what will happen in your old age. The most immediate effect, though, is of course that neither of us has to work any more. I still wake up every morning feeling grateful for that. Not that I hated my work, you understand, but I realize now how little freedom you have as an employee. There is always someone you have to say yes to, always somewhere you have to be at a certain time, always something that has to be done by a certain date, and of course most jobs are so boring as well. You do it because you need the money but you never have time to enjoy any of it because you spend so much of your time working that you're exhausted by the time you get home. The only time you get off is the week-end, when the roads are jammed, and two weeks in the summer when everything is crowded with other holidaymakers. You can't go far enough to find somewhere quiet because there isn't enough time to make it worthwhile. So you have to wait until you retire and then of course you can't afford it. It really is a very stupid system. I don't think many people ever look at it like that—I know I didn't—but of course even if they did they couldn't do much about it. That's why the football pools are so popular you see, it's the only way out for people like us.

'In fact, you know, I wrote a book about how to win money on the pools while I was on this cruise. It took me about three weeks but my wife won't let me publish it until I win again. She thinks that if I can get two big wins then the book will sell better. She's probably right, but I would still do the pools every week whether I'd written this book or not. It would be lovely to win again. I suppose it's a question of the more you have the more you want. I really feel now that one *needs* this sort of money to live properly today. I can't think how we managed before.

'One thing I'm very grateful for is that we have both been able to handle it. I know of so many people who have been completely destroyed by winning a fortune on the pools—either they end up on a psychiatrist's couch or else they just give the stuff away because they can't cope with it. I think in our case we had dreamed about it for such a long time that we more or less went ahead and turned our dreams into reality.'

Betty comes in bearing a tray of steaming coffee and, after administering milk and sugar, settles herself on a stool by the fire to join in the conversation.

'What I don't know,' she declares happily, 'is how we ever had the time to go to work. There's so much to do in the house, and of course we entertain a lot now. Last weekend we had fourteen people to stay, and though that is rather an exception there's usually someone dropping in most days. I do all the work myself, me and Madge that is, because I suppose I'm used to it and anyway it would be so expensive having someone living in. We had the windows cleaned the other day, and do you know it cost us £3 just for that! I told Joe he ought to take up window-cleaning and never mind about doing the pools.

'I'm sorry in a way that we didn't win this money about twenty years ago—we would really have gone on a spending spree then. I think when you're young you have a different attitude to things like security, and of course you're not so set in your ways. I enjoy spending the money, of course I do, but I'm not at all extravagant with it. I still buy my clothes at C & A for example—I'd much rather have more cheap things than a few expensive ones. It's the same with food. I buy more food rather than better food. One thing I did enjoy though was buying things for the house. It was so lovely to be able to choose the things that we liked rather than the things we could afford, that really was nice.

'Do we feel different? Well, yes, in a way I suppose we do. There's none of the worry about where the next penny is coming from and whether or not we can afford to have someone round for dinner tomorrow night. I'm certainly conscious of the fact that we're in the money now. I would never tell the neighbours about it for example because I know what it's like to feel you can't keep up with someone richer than yourself, I know it would embarrass them terribly. The only people we enjoy showing off to are the ones who used to impress us with their money—it's nice to be able to turn the tables on them.

'But it certainly hasn't changed us in a fundamental sense. We still have the same friends, still go down to the pub two or three times a week. Even the cruise was an exception really; we've now got a cottage on the coast and when it's nice or when we want a change we go and stay down there for a bit.

'I think we both felt a bit sorry at first that we didn't have any children to enjoy all this money with us, but really you know with all the things you read in the papers about kids these days taking drugs and fixing themselves and so on we feel that perhaps it's turned out for the best after all. We do have lots of animals—three dogs, two cats, a budgerigar and a couple of goldfish—and really they are such good company that we never miss not having any children around the house.

'All the same, since we don't have any children we feel that we would like the money to do some good after we're gone. First of all it will go to Madge of course, but after that we have made arrangements for it to be left to hospitals and nursing associations. In fact you know if we ever won the pools again I think we would give most of it to the hospitals straight away. After all they are really helping everyone, aren't they, so the money would really be going to everybody in need.

'Of course, to be quite honest, it's impossible to say what we would really do if we won that amount of money a second time. Money does strange things to you. This might sound peculiar but in spite of all that we have, I still dream of having a lot more money. Perhaps everyone has dreams like that, no matter how rich they are. But in spite of that I do realize that the important thing is to have enough money to be free, to be your own boss and arrange your life the way you want it. Once you have achieved that then anything more is really superfluous.'

Not everyone would agree with that, of course. Many people are of the opinion that it is only after escaping from the burden of financial necessity that one can begin to live at all. In the rarefied atmosphere of monetary plenty, anything is possible—glamour, luxury, comfort, popularity, even longevity—for once the element of worry has been removed life takes on a completely different flavour and self-indulgence is not slow to set in. Still it is the first benefit, release from worry, which causes people in their thousands to envy the Donalds, and although the likelihood of a substantial win is remote indeed, the coupons are filled in week after week by hopeful contenders.

This spirit of optimism pervades all forms of gambling, and where players can risk unlimited stakes it is a factor which can lead to total disaster. In fact, gambling rarely makes dreams come true and in some cases it can even turn into an unforgettable nightmare.

Part Two

CRAVING MONEY

CHAPTER THREE

Gambling

The glittering attractions of gambling are open to all comers. In a world in which most of us dream of being rich and few of us succeed, it is hardly surprising that the number of those who come is increasing steadily. For there is little chance of successfully working one's way to a million under the present tax system, and even less chance of inheriting a fortune from an unknown relative. The only real hope of escaping from one's financial rut, therefore, is to gamble one's way out of it.

This is not the only reason for trying one's luck, for the rich gamble as much as the poor. But whether it is the glint of gold or just the thrill of the game, there are few people today who do not gamble on something at some time in their lives, and for many it is a regular habit like smoking or drinking. It is so much a part of everyday life that one tends to forget that in Britain today's major industry is less than fifteen years old. For gambling did not become respectable until 1960, when the Betting and Gaming Act brought it within the framework of the law and paved the way for the introduction of betting shops. The social stigma so long attached to gambling gradually began to fade, and the betting shop, like the pub before it and the sex shop after it, took its place as an accepted part of the high street scene. The boom triggered off by the 1960 Act of Parliament is now a multi-million-pound industry and any reservations that may linger in the minds of puritans are eclipsed by money-making pursuits such as bingo and premium bonds which have firmly established gambling as a respectable middle-class institution. Now, in theory at least, anyone can become a millionaire overnight.

The fantasy element is of course a major attraction. In an age in which fantasy is increasingly hard to come by, the vision of passing from rags to riches overnight is plainly irresistible. This is a factor exploited to the full in the publicity given to those lucky few who do manage to hit the jackpot. Any major win on the football pools is treated as a subject of national importance, with headlines splashed across the front page and an attention to detail usually reserved for politicians, film stars and royalty. The following is an extract from a typical press report of a record pools payout in November 1971*:

> 'Sixty-one-year-old pit worker Jack Heald, in London today to pick up a pools cheque for £247,659.70, ordered two 7p hot dogs at King's Cross station when he arrived and said, "Who's going to pay?" At the time he was facing a battery of photographers. "Well," he repeated, "who's going to pay . . . me or you?"
>
> 'Then on second thoughts he dipped into his pocket and handed the 14p over the station cafeteria counter . . .
>
> 'On-top-of-the-world Yorkshireman Mr Heald . . . a miner for 35 years, said "We couldn't believe it. This will mean I can retire and it's a wonderful way to do it."'

The fever is catching, and one tends to forget that for every Mr Heald there are thousands who pay their money and lose. Businessmen and governments, however, have been far from slow to see and exploit the potential of gambling, and the business of making money out of other

* *London Evening Standard.*

people's desire to make money is positively booming.

The current growth and profitability of the gambling industry is partly due to the ease and speed of the whole operation. A punter with a credit account has his information available on the end of a telephone line, while the man in a betting shop can watch the situation for himself, listen to the result over the shop's loudspeaker and collect his winnings within minutes. The success of the system is reflected in the cool £120 million a year that is currently being poured into the ever-open arms of the Exchequer in the form of betting tax.

The introduction of betting shops was undoubtedly the best thing that ever happened to the gambling industry. All the big operators are expanding this side of their business as fast as they can, and in view of the fact that three-quarters of Ladbrokes' £80 million annual turnover comes from their 700-odd betting shops, one can see why.

The brief history of the gambling industry is studded with profits all the way along the line. People seem peculiarly anxious to part with their money, even in times of severe economic depression and hardship, for even then the rate of gambling continues unabated. Presumably it provides an escape from reality, and when things are bad the need to escape becomes even more acute. Also, of course, gambling supplies an element of hope—to try one's luck is at least to have a chance of winning, and that thought alone helps to lighten the weight of one's worries. There is a saying in the gambling business that 'no-one ever commits suicide with an ante-post voucher in his pocket',* and it is this magical vision of next time that keeps the money flowing, not only on the race track and in the

* An ante-post voucher is a bet on a future event.

casinos but everywhere where there is the possibility of making a kill.

This instinct to gamble is the key to the industry's success. The demand is already there—all the bookmaker has to do is to satisfy it by providing the necessary facilities. The odds are of course adjusted in his favour to reduce his risk to a minimum, and bookmakers' profits do not depend to any great extent on the outcome of races. Of course there are bad days, but these tend to even out over a period and the percentage profit does not vary very much.

In spite of the fact that most of the industry's £1,000 million turnover is accounted for by takings on horses and dogs, people can and do bet on almost anything. Political elections, in particular, have become a favourite target for speculation, and the biggest amount of money ever taken by Ladbrokes on a single event was the £1,600,000 that came pouring in on the 1964 general election. Other favourites are the annual Miss World contest, the elusive Loch Ness monster and the space race. One Birmingham bookmaker will even give you odds on the vagaries of the English weather.

The increasing popularity of this type of fringe betting is a reflection of the ease with which publicity can create demand. Ladbrokes were the first firm to arouse an interest in political betting, just as they created a national flood of interest in the escape of Goldie the eagle by offering odds as to the length of time he would be able to avoid recapture. Betting of this kind is really entertainment; and by first creating and then satisfying the demand bookmakers hope to extend their list of clients by appealing to a wider section of the community. Many people who would never dream of laying money on a horse, for example, would be quite prepared to have a flutter on the general election. Women, too, are more likely to be attracted by the idea of Goldie the eagle than by the 3.15 at Epsom. On the whole, though, women are not attracted to gambling and the number of women who gamble with any regularity is negligible. There is, however, one important exception where women outnumber men by about two to one, and that exception is bingo.

Bingo today is peculiarly British, as British as fish and chips and bowler hats, yet strangely enough the game did not originate in this country but in seventeenth-century Italy. It was known for a long time as Lotto, but the name changed as the habit spread. Twentieth-century Americans christened it Keno, in Ireland it was known as Pongo, while in Britain, under the name of Housey Housey, it was the only gambling game permitted in the armed services. It has been suggested that the reason for this was that it was introduced to familiarize illiterate soldiers with numbers. All in all, its origins are far from illustrious, yet from these humble beginnings there has grown an astonishing industry which now boasts a total turnover of more than £250 million a year.

Commercial bingo did not appear in Britain until 1960 when the Betting and Gaming Act provided for the first time for the creation of clubs devoted entirely to this form of gambling. There are now, at the time of writing, about 1,700 such clubs throughout the country, and indeed the enthusiasm with which the British took up the craze was little less than phenomenal. Bingo in the early '60s was a magic word. It appeared regularly in the headlines not only as a rapidly growing industry but as a national characteristic. No study of the British nation at that time was complete without a reference to its current fascination with the numbers game of clickety click, Kelly's eye, and legs eleven.

The fact that bingo now appears rarely in the press does not mean that it has fallen out of favour; on the contrary its lack of news value is an indication of the extent to which it has become a part of the British way of life. Bingo has effectively filled the gap left by the disappearance of the music hall and the decline of the cinema as a source of entertainment. In fact if there had not been such a considerable number of cinemas up for sale, it is doubtful whether bingo would have met with the measure of success it has.

As it was, bingo fans multiplied daily. The audiences that came pouring into the bingo halls in the early days consisted mainly of people in the lower income groups—the traditional bingo player was working class, upwards of middle-aged, and female. Apart from the fact that the average age has now come down to between 35 and 50, audience composition has changed very little over the years. Bingo fans are still predominately working class, and women still make up the majority, between 60% and 70%.

The attraction of the bingo hall, like that of the music hall that preceded it, lies primarily in the atmosphere of social togetherness it sets out to promote. By providing drinks and refreshments, friendly chat and sponsored outings, the bingo halls seem more like social clubs than gambling parlours. This seems to account for the high proportion of women players, most of whom have little opportunity to escape from the tediousness of their domestic routine. The bingo hall provides a place where they can relax, drink, and meet their friends, not forgetting the added attraction of possibly walking out a few hundred pounds richer at the end of the evening.

The money element is certainly important, even if the most one can hope to win is only £1000. After all the stakes are small, about 50p for a book of tickets, and even an average win of £300 to £400 is well worthwhile at that kind of price. Obviously bingo is not a game for hardened gamblers, but that does not make it any the less serious for those who do indulge in it. Those who say that bingo is not a serious game should sit in on one or two sessions and watch the intense concentration on the faces of those taking part. The involvement is so complete that when, on one occasion, a player collapsed in the middle of a game and had to be rushed to hospital, the only emotion registered by his fellow players was extreme irritability at the interruption of the game. On another occasion a boatload of bingo players heading for Ostend came across a ship in distress. In spite of the urgent mayday call, not a single player could be found even to come up on deck let alone offer to lend a hand. It is in the light of total and frightening detachment such as this that one begins to understand something of the problems of the compulsive gambler.

The compulsive gambler is still very much an outcast in the eyes of society, partly because his existence has only recently come to light and partly because his total failure with regard to matters of money tends to arouse contempt rather than compassion. In fact, of course, compulsive gambling is a disease, a particularly horrifying kind of disease which inevitably leaves in its wake a trail of misery, destruction and torment. No-one knows this better than Sally who, at 46, has been married to a compulsive gambler for twenty-four years. A frail but intense woman, her unkempt brown hair streaked with grey and her face pale and deeply drawn, Sally lives with her husband and two children in a sparsely furnished council house in South London. Yet in spite of their obvious poverty and the pain that shadows her face as she talks of her past life, she radiates a warmth and a strength that invite sympathy rather than pity. This is her story, told in the hope that it may serve as a warning to others and in doing so give them the courage to act before it is too late.

'My first indication of what was to come came about a week before we were due to be married when John disappeared without a trace. I didn't see or hear anything of him for three days, and I was on the point of cancelling the wedding altogether when he reappeared as suddenly as he had left. All he said was that he had been gambling to try and make some money and that he'd gambled all our savings away.

'Well it was just after the war and no-one had any money anyway, so apart from the fact that it seemed a rather silly thing to have done it didn't really bother me very much. I convinced John that it wasn't important and that we should go ahead and everything would be all right. So we got married.

'We had managed to get hold of a little house in South London, simply because the owner took a liking to us. You couldn't get a house for love or money in those days, and at first things really did seem to be all right. We were both working; John was teaching and earning enough money to pay the bills and repay his debts, and I had an office job to cover the cost of the housekeeping.

'But then things began to go wrong. John started staying out at night, sometimes not coming home until the early hours of the morning, sometimes not coming home at all. He tried to convince me that he kept meeting up with friends from his army days, but when he started to come home drunk and even stayed away at week-ends I thought that perhaps he was turning into an alcoholic. Sometimes he even beat me up. I had absolutely no way of knowing that he spent all his spare time gambling and that he drank to try and forget how much he had lost. Even if I had known I don't suppose I would have been able to cope. I was very young and very naïve, so I just tried to believe what he told me in the hope that things would improve on their own.

'They didn't of course, and two years after our marriage I had a breakdown and ended up in hospital. I found no help there at all—the doctors and I just couldn't communicate—and in the end I discharged myself and went back home. I can't blame the people there. They were as ignorant of compulsive gambling as I was. Anyway, when I recovered, John and I decided to have a baby and somehow that decision brought a period of calm to our relationship.

'The following summer Marion was born, and on the day John was supposed to come and collect us from the hospital he disappeared. I remember watching all the other young mothers, happy and smiling as they went off home with their husbands. I remember waiting for my turn to come and feeling my own happiness slowly turning into despair and disbelief as I realized that he wasn't coming after all. In the end I went home alone. The house was empty and there was no trace of John anywhere.

'The next day he just turned up, saying that he had got caught up at a race meeting and couldn't make it. I was hurt and confused, but at the same time I was so relieved to see him that I didn't ask any questions. Six months later he forged a cheque.

'The scandal was terrible. We lived in a small suburban community, and before long it was all over the front page of the local paper. John was prosecuted, he lost his job and on top of it our landlord politely asked us to leave. We lost everything—our house, our belongings, our livelihood, our reputation—and all because of £12, that's the irony of it.

'For the next two years we lived apart, we had no choice. Marion and I went to stay with my mother in her two-roomed cottage, and John had to find lodgings. It was terrible. I took a job as soon as I could and when I had saved enough money I began to look for somewhere for the three of us to live. It was marvellous when I found a furnished house that we could afford, but we hardly spent six months there because John began forging the rent book and we were evicted.

'This time I felt unable to ask my mother for help. John disappeared again and I was left penniless with Marion. I finally ended up in a rest centre full of drug addicts, drop outs and alcoholics. About a month later Marion became very ill, and my mother came and took us home.

'I was still convinced in my heart that John and I could start again. I never stopped loving him and I always knew that he loved me, in spite of what other people said. So I found another job and about a year later I managed to get a council house. That was really fantastic. We borrowed £20 for a deposit on some furniture and we became a family again.

'When Marion was three years old John insisted on having another child. I didn't want to, not because I didn't want any more—I love children—but because I thought it was the wrong time. I wanted us to settle a bit more first. We had had so much upheaval and insecurity, and I felt we needed more time to grow together again. Anyway we had a terrible row about it and in the end I gave in.

'Soon after Martin was born John suddenly announced that he was going to emigrate to Canada. I just couldn't believe it. We argued and rowed about it for weeks, but John was so sure that everything would be all right and that he would establish himself sufficiently for us to be able to join him inside a year that I finally agreed. I agreed, not because I thought it was the right thing to do, but because I felt he would always hold it against me if I refused. He left when Martin was just three months old, saying that there was enough money in the bank to look after our immediate needs and that he would be sending money from Canada.

'Of course there was no money at all—in fact there wasn't even a bank account. He had left us literally without a single penny. This time I had to get national assistance, as it was then. I gave up the house and moved with the children into a prefab.

'During those months I starved. I couldn't work because the baby was too small to be left, and I had no income at all. I borrowed money from my mother to buy food for the children, that was as much as I could bring myself to do. I often wonder what all those civilized people who were so horrified at the forging of a cheque would have said if they had known that their nextdoor neighbour was suffering from malnutrition. I'm quite sure they wouldn't have put *that* on the front page of the local paper. Society has strange values when it comes to money.

'Anyway soon after that I contracted polio, and after about eighteen months John finally came home—or rather my brother paid the fare to bring him home. I discovered later that he had gambled his way right across Canada, leaving a trail of debts behind him. He hadn't a penny in his pocket when he came back.

'I took another job as soon as I could, and John started teaching again. I worked in the evenings while John was supposedly babysitting. Thank God I never knew that he was in fact out gambling every night, and that the children were alone in an empty house. I can't bring myself to think about it even now. It never occurred to me that he might be gambling because there was no money to gamble with. In fact John had embezzled about £350 from the school funds and it wasn't long before the theft was discovered and he disappeared yet again.

'Somehow we managed to avoid a second prosecution, but John's teaching career was finished and we were evicted from the prefab. It seems incredible, looking back, but even then I didn't know what the problem was. I thought John's gambling was the outcome of the situation we were in, not the cause of it. More than anything I thought that there was something wrong with me, that I was inadequate in some way.

'During the next two years John didn't work at all and I had to earn the money to keep us. Martin was then six and Marion nine. Eventually John did manage to find another teaching job, but even with both of us working there were constant money problems, bills that couldn't be paid, debts that never diminished, and still John drank and still he gambled.

'When she was twelve years old, Marion won a scholarship to a public school. She had always been a bright child and we were delighted. In some ways though it was hard, with school uniform to buy and the constant strain of making sure that she didn't stand out from the other girls, most of whom came from well-off, middle-class homes. It was a strain on her, too, because the pressure of her school work came at a time when she was old enough to realize what was going on at home. When she was fifteen she tried to commit suicide ... She's twenty-two now with a good university degree and soon she'll be getting married. Martin is eighteen and studying to be a barrister.

'They've been marvellous children, both of them, but of course they've suffered. We all have. We never had a holiday together, not once. I never even managed to take the children down to the sea for a day. John's suffered too of course. His gambling has lost him his self-respect and the respect of his children, and that's one of the worst things that can happen to a man. As for me, it's made me lose every bit of feeling I ever had for money or nice things. Money is just paper to me, paper to pay bills with so that the bailiffs don't come and throw us out of our home, paper to provide the necessities of life, to keep us together as a family. The ironical thing is that money means nothing at all to John, in spite of the fortune that has passed through his hands since he started gambling. To him money is just the tool he needs to satisfy his craving for betting, that's all.

'Not that I blame John for what's happened to us, I've never blamed him. The people I hold responsible are the ones who promote gambling and grow rich on the proceeds. John's weakness would never have had such terrible consequences if others hadn't made it so easy for him. Why, people are positively encouraged to gamble, to win, to envy those who win a fortune on the pools. The pursuit of money has been exaggerated and exploited beyond all reason, and people don't realize what it can turn into until it is too late.

'One thing that our experience has done for me is strengthen my belief in God, if only because I'm convinced that there's got to be a better life than this somewhere.

Would I have married John if I'd known what was to come? I'd be a fool if I said yes, nobody would. A gambler's life is worse than a drug addict's; a drug addict can at least hope to die young, but a gambler can only live a life of hell—and believe me, it is hell—until he dies.'

Sally and John are now members of Gamblers Anonymous, and for the first time they have found real friendship and understanding among others who share the same problem. Compulsive gambling is spreading with frightening speed. It claims addicts from all walks of life, doctors, bus drivers, priests, teachers, even housewives who regularly spend all their housekeeping money on bingo. Disturbingly it also claims a growing number of youngsters barely out of school. An increasing number of bewildered mothers are bringing their sons, aged 17 and 18, to Gamblers Anonymous in the hope that something can be done to help them before they ruin their own lives and the lives of those who become involved with them. Sometimes it is possible to cure them, often it is not. Temptation is always so close at hand—there is a betting shop in almost every High Street, often placed without thought near social security offices or council housing estates. The social climate implicitly encourages gambling by glorifying gain and minimizing effort, and of course it is not to be overlooked that those who would be in a position to reduce the volume of gambling are precisely those who have the most to gain from it.

Money breeds money, how true it is; but it is sad to think that so much effort and so much money should be involved in the creation of a major industry with no end product. For gambling *is* a totally non-productive exercise; it does not improve the mind or gladden the heart. It is there simply to empty some people's pockets and fill others.

It seems a poor justification for the destruction and human misery endured by Sally and others like her, no matter how small the percentage of gamblers they represent.

Making money, however, is often a sordid business. The lengths to which people are prepared to go vary according to their individual character and the atmosphere of the times, but most of them still stop short of breaking the law. When John's obsession with gambling drove him to crime it was out of desperation and, being on unfamiliar ground, he was not very successful at it. The following section looks at some of the professionals who spend their whole lives in the shadows, those whose self-appointed job is to make crime pay.

Part Three

MONEY THROUGH CRIME

CHAPTER FOUR

Theft

In 1971 the number of cases of theft, robbery and burglary known to have been committed in London alone rose to a total of just under 256,000. The true figure was of course very much higher, but whatever the real picture for that year one thing remains certain. None of those crimes was committed by Maureen O'Hara, for Maureen was then doing time in Holloway jail.

Maureen O'Hara is a thief. The youngest of seventeen children, she started stealing when she was only twelve years old. Now, at fifty, she has spent twenty years of her life behind bars, and it shows. Her face is drawn and haggard without a trace of colour, her wiry grey hair is thinning fast, and during her last jail sentence she lost over twenty-five pounds in weight. Her body is shrunken as well as emaciated and she looks and walks like a woman of seventy. Physically she is a wreck. Yet Maureen, who now lives in a small, cramped hostel inhabited mostly by drug addicts and alcoholics, has surprisingly few regrets about her life of crime. In fact her eyes, fiercely bright and exceptionally blue, leave one in little doubt that, if necessary, she would be quite prepared to do the same thing all over again.

'My father was an alcoholic and my mother killed herself when I was fourteen. It was the drinking that drove her to it, she just couldn't cope with that and the seventeen of us as well.

'We lived in Liverpool at the time and soon after my mother died I started housebreaking together with a girl-friend. It was exciting I suppose, but looking back it was really very small-time stealing. We used to spend the money on clothes until we were caught. Being the last of seventeen kids I never had any new clothes—everything was handed down—and when you're fourteen or fifteen nice things begin to matter to you. I didn't feel guilty about stealing, I looked on it as a game more than anything else. But being caught made it all much more serious. I was sent to approved school and then to borstal where I learnt much more about crime than I could ever have picked up on my own. Borstal is about the best training ground anyone could have.

'When war broke out in 1945 I got a job in a parachute factory. It was difficult for me to get work because I lost an eye in a firework accident when I was a kid. I sometimes think that if I hadn't had that accident I might not have started stealing, but I know it isn't true. Stealing is easier than working.

'I suppose that having my brothers and sisters working as well should really have made it easier for me but in fact it made no difference at all. I've always been lazy, ever since I can remember, and having found a way of making a few hundred quid in a few hours made it very difficult to come to terms with working a whole week for less than £10. It didn't seem right, and before long I just came to the conclusion that working was a waste of time, particularly as the jobs I had were so boring anyway.

'When the war ended I came to London where I lived on national assistance in between pulling jobs. I had made enough contacts in borstal to be able to off-load the stuff without any trouble, though of course with stolen goods you can't be too fussy about the price. The cash you end up with is nowhere near the real value of the stuff, and, knowing they have you over a barrel, some dealers really squeeze you hard. All the same it's easy to knock up a few hundred quid a week and sometimes it can be a lot more than that, especially if you're lucky enough to come across a pile of cash in a drawer somewhere. People never bother to take down the numbers of their notes and you can just go out and blow it without worrying. It was a carefree kind of life when I had no-one but myself to look after, but I don't think I ever thought of it as something I would do for the rest of my life. I took it for granted that when I got married I would give it up, and I'm sure I could have gone straight if I'd married the right man. Unfortunately the one I ended up with, an Irishman, turned out to be an alcoholic like my father. Instead of working to keep me he lived off other Irishmen who gave him money whenever they had any to spare. Sean has never done a day's work in his life; he lives for his drink, that's all. Soon I had eight children to support and with no money coming in I had no choice but to go back to crime. It was the only thing I knew how to do.

'I don't regret it. I did it for my children, so that they could be well dressed and properly fed. I never thought about the people I was stealing from, I just knew that my family needed money and that other people could provide it. I suppose it's selfish, but then everyone is selfish nowadays. I never had a conscience about what I was doing, not until I came face to face with the people in the dock. Then when you see them as individuals you realize that they've worked hard for what they've got. Perhaps the fur coat or piece of jewellery was an anniversary present saved up for over a long period of time. You feel really sorry when you're in court but it still doesn't stop you doing the same thing again as soon as you get out. When you're desperate you see, you convince yourself that they couldn't possibly need it as much as you do.

'Most people who get robbed are insured anyway so it doesn't really hurt them, does it? I remember I once took about £2,000 worth of stuff from a businessman's home, and I heard later that he had got £5,000 out of his insurance company. Well I'd like to know who was the bigger crook, him or me.

'In any case, how many people can honestly say they've never cheated anyone else? They don't like to admit it but they're all at it to some extent. Either they fiddle their employer or they fiddle the state or they leave their bills unpaid ... not many can say no to making a bit on the side. It's the atmosphere we live in—you can't do anything without money and if you don't look after yourself no-one else will.

'I must say I was a lazy burglar though. I never bothered to find out about the people whose homes I broke into—I just picked the ones that looked most inviting. So many people leave their windows open or doors unlocked when they go out. Housebreaking really couldn't be easier, especially in London.

'Sometimes you make mistakes of course. Once, when I was working with another girl we lifted a safe from this very plush private house. It was so heavy we could hardly lift it between us, but we were so sure of being able to retire on the proceeds that we really didn't care. We bribed a taxi driver to take us out of town to the nearest bit of woodland and he even helped us to get the safe into a clearing when we got there. He was a nice bloke, I can still see him now. Anyway when we finally blew this thing open we found out why it was so heavy. The damn thing was stuffed full of nails and screws. We honestly didn't know whether to laugh or cry.

'Another time I remember is when I was working on my own and I got into this very posh house through an open window. The first place to make for of course is the master bedroom and I was just in the middle of gathering stuff together when I heard a key in the front door downstairs. There was no way for me to get out, so quick as a flash I jumped into the wardrobe hoping that whoever it was might go out again. Just my luck of course the first thing that Madam did was come upstairs to hang her coat in the wardrobe. She nearly had a fit when she saw me in there. "What on earth are you doing?" she bleated. I looked her straight in the eye, and cool as a cucumber I said, "O don't worry about me love, I'm just waiting for a bus." That cost me five years inside that did.

'My children always came to see me when I was inside, regular as clockwork. They never held it against me, they knew I only did it for them. They're wonderful, my kids, they'd follow me anywhere. The eldest ones are eighteen now, twin girls, and they've both got marvellous jobs. One works for the civil service and the other is a typist in a big London store. They wouldn't dream of getting into trouble, it just wouldn't enter their heads. I did have a bit of trouble with one of the younger ones but I took her to a child psychiatrist and she's all right now. All the younger kids are in care at the moment but I hope that I'll be able to get a job this time and have them back. The twins don't give me any money and I wouldn't dream of asking them; they work hard for what they earn and I'm happy to see them spend it on themselves. Anyway the council is trying to find us a house now so that we can all live together again.

'I did try to go straight from time to time but with only national assistance to live on and my husband insisting on £1 a day for drink it never lasted very long. I wanted to leave him, it got so bad, but when I went to the priest to ask him for help in getting a separation he told me I should try and carry on. I think that's what turned me against religion. When the kids were starving he had nothing to say, the good priest. The only advice he offered was to go to church and pray, and every time I went to church what happened? They passed an enormous plate round and urged us to put in notes instead of silver. I'm through with religion. If I wanted to break into a house and steal something God wouldn't suddenly appear in front of me and stop me doing it. I don't believe in an after-life either, or that I shall be punished for the way I've lived. I did it to get money for my children, and if there is a God then he must know that.

'Funnily enough I was never put off by the thought of going back inside. Prison is too soft; it's more like a convalescent home than a deterrent really, what with radios, record players, curtains and so on. The only difference is that you can't walk out of the front gate. I think twenty years is enough though. I'm really determined to get a job and go straight this time.

'Money is such a curse. If only one could manage without it I would never have seen the inside of a prison cell. I know one can work for it and that lots of people do work very hard but I'm not cut out for that kind of life. The money I've earned certainly feels different from the money I've stolen and it's nice not to have to worry about suddenly having a hand on your shoulder, but even so I could never have been a donkey all my life. (That's what we call those who do the nine-to-five routine, donkeys.) I must say I'm glad my kids won't have to go through what I've been through. Jail can break you if you're sensitive.

'I think the worst part of prison life is all the goings on in there. I didn't know what lesbian meant until I went to jail. They're all so blatant about it too—a mate of mine once asked me to do her a favour and take round the porridge as she had something pressing to do. I didn't mind so I said yes, and when I got to her cell there she was, large as life, carrying on with another prisoner. I was so furious I poured the porridge over both their heads.

'It's not only the prisoners either, the officers join in as well. It's easy to buy favours with a bit of sex, or with money if you have it. I remember that one officer was dismissed for carrying on with a lifer, but that was only because someone reported it and they had to do something about it. As far as I can see there are more bent officers than straight ones anyway. It's hardly the kind of atmosphere to encourage you to go straight, what with that and the number of tips you pick up. I know I'm not really a very good advert myself since I never managed to stay out for more than a few months at a time, but I know plenty of people who do. Prison teaches you a lot, but like everything else you have to be able to apply it. I suppose I'm just not a very good crook.

'At least my brothers and sisters have been spared the shame of knowing how I've lived. I hardly ever see them, you see, and I don't think they even realize that I've been in jail. They can't do because the other day I had a letter from my sister saying that she was about to be evicted and could I possibly send her some money. They all live in the north you see, and they think that just because I'm in London I must be well off. I suppose it's a bit of a sick joke really.

'It's funny, but money really means nothing to me now that the kids are old enough to look after themselves. I suppose that if I'd known how to handle it, invested it or something instead of just spending it, I might have been able to give up thieving a long time ago and live on the proceeds instead. I must say, though, that looking back over my life I feel I've achieved a lot, even if other people may not think so. I have a fine family who are a credit to me and to society as well. They may not have grown up in ideal circumstances, but they've turned out all right in spite of that. Surely it was better for me to steal in order to give them the best I could rather than run the risk of all of them turning into criminals. Having nothing is much worse than having a thief as a mother. I must say though that if I lived my life over again I wouldn't do the same thing—they say that Barclaycards are very much easier.'

Indeed for those who are clever enough to master the finer points, fraud is very much easier. Not only is there less risk of being caught because fewer clues are left behind, but the conman does not even have the worry of selling off stolen goods. If he knows what he is doing, a clever operator can make thousands of pounds for himself without too much trouble and without anyone being any the wiser.

CHAPTER FIVE

Fraud

Unlike the burglar, blackmailer, or violent criminal, the conman does not lurk in the shadowy horror chambers of the mind. His particular gift for extracting money causes neither pain nor fear, he sheds no blood and takes no life. It is for this reason that fraud is looked upon as a relatively harmless crime, and if it arouses any emotion at all the most likely one is sneaking admiration. To take money, particularly from those who can afford it such as governments, banks and corporations, by using brainpower rather than physical violence, is something that few people will find repugnant. Money, after all, is replaceable, human life is not.

The relative lack of concern caused by bloodless crimes such as fraud is only one reason why this kind of activity is booming as never before. Other factors, such as the understandable reluctance of victims to admit that they have been fooled and the harassment of an already overworked and undermanned police force for whom all but the most serious of fraud cases must rate as minor offences, combine to make the life of a conman increasingly attractive. It is not difficult to clear a few thousand pounds a year free of tax, and if the police do get to hear about it the chances of detection are slight enough to make the risk well worth taking.

This is not a sign of incompetence on the part of the police force; it is an indication of an impossible situation.

In London alone the number of known fraud cases rose by 23.4% during 1972 to a total of well over 25,000. Since the majority of crimes go unreported, the true picture is very much more serious, and there is no doubt that this area of crime is increasing at a much faster rate than others. While it is true that every large town has its own specially trained Fraud Squad, this still leaves large areas of the British Isles quite unprepared for the investigation of crimes of this kind. Time is a vital factor, and the time taken by a rural officer to conduct a preliminary investigation and pass on the facts to the nearest Fraud Squad can make all the difference when it comes to trailing a fast-moving conman.

But that is only the beginning of the problem. Many instances of fraud and white-collar crime involve highly complicated mathematical manoeuvres that are quite beyond the comprehension of anyone without an advanced knowledge of accountancy. The conman who is skilled in the finer points of high finance has the edge over everyone all along the line, for even if the police do formulate a charge against him and take him to court it is unlikely that the average jury will fully understand what he has been up to. A doubtful jury will usually play safe and return a verdict of not guilty, so that even at this stage the criminal can still go free.

Fraud does not have to be complicated; in fact it can sometimes be very simple indeed. One of the simplest and most common confidence tricks is to dress up something worthless and pass it off as a desirable acquisition. Anything will do, even acorns, as was proved by the advertisement in a gardening magazine urging enthusiasts to grow 'your own exotic Japanese oaks from pedigree acorns collected by qualified plant hunters'. Few gardeners could resist, and the advertisement produced hundreds of 50p postal orders in the first week. The acorns were duly dispatched, and it was not until a suspicious recipient sent his budding Japanese oak down to the Royal Horticultural Society for examination that the truth was discovered, the truth being of course that the acorns had been patiently gathered from parks and gardens around London. Possibly 50p may not seem very much to those who are accustomed to thinking in thousands, but when multiplied by six or seven hundred it is still not a bad return on the cost of a single advertisement.

It is not difficult to think of variations on this theme, such as maps revealing buried treasure on non-existent islands or worthless deeds to plots of land in the Caribbean. Sometimes the man behind the advertisement does not bother to reply at all—he simply collects the money and moves on. By the time his victims have realized what has happened and reported it to the police, he is nowhere to be found. He has moved, changed his name and set up in a new district, ready to pull the same hoax once more.

Tricks such as these add up to very small-time fraud, requiring little intelligence and involving a minimum of risk. The amount of effort involved in tracing this kind of hoaxer and bringing him to justice is generally out of proportion to the scale of his activities. But if it is safe to be small, it is probably even safer to be big. The barrister who sold several hundred defective tractors to the Chinese Communist government on behalf of one of Britain's most respected companies was well aware of this as he pocketed his cheque for £15,500. He received a second cheque a few months later for selling them a million pounds' worth of spare parts, and at that stage he and his wife quietly withdrew to live abroad. Fraud on this scale, were it ever to come to light, would be far too big to prosecute.

Respectability is undoubtedly an asset for anyone contemplating breaking the law, and many people who indulge in fraud and white-collar crime are respectable up to the hilt. Those who are not will often appear to be so, an easy enough task when anyone can set up and register a company for as little as £25 and become a company director overnight. Incredible though it may seem, the accepted image of a company director is still that of a man of integrity and substance. The main advantage of respectability is that it enables one to raise credit, and credit, more than any other single factor, is the backbone of fraud. A ghostly company with impressive notepaper can obtain goods on credit, sell them for cash, and even raise and withdraw money from several banks before fading gently into oblivion.

Many conmen, however, do have extremely good jobs with high salaries and sound prospects. The reason why they are not satisfied is that, at the present time, a good job with a high salary and sound prospects means something in the region of £5,000 a year with a pension on retirement. An efficient conman can make three or four times that amount with a minimum of sweat and no income tax to pay. If he keeps his job as well, and arranges for his extra funds to be channelled into a numbered account in Switzerland then he has the best of both worlds.

Nor, in all fairness, can he be blamed. The principle of more and more money for less and less effort is well established and the blaze of publicity given to pay rise announcements serves to keep discontent simmering among the community at large. Everyone is out for as much as he can get, and if he can get it while giving little or nothing in return so much the better.

Not surprisingly, the habit of getting something for nothing is now being adopted by children too. A survey carried out in 1969 by the Surrey Research Centre of the London School of Economics under the direction of Dr W. A. Belsen revealed the following startling facts: a total of 89% of London boys in the 13–16 year age group said that they had at some time kept things which they had found; 63% admitted stealing school property; 51% said that they had stolen money. The findings are endorsed by the 1972 report of the Commissioner of Police which shows that young people in the 10–20 year age group were responsible for nearly half the indictable offences committed in London, with offenders between the ages of 14 and 16 accounting for over 18% of all arrests. Worse still, the number of crimes committed by 10-year-olds rose by 14.5% during the year to a total of well over 1,000. Children, particularly children of that age, must learn from what they see and hear around them, and the implications for society as a whole are deeply disturbing.

It is worth noting, in passing, that while dishonesty is universal, fraud and white-collar crime appear to flourish in capitalist societies only, where swindling the state in particular has become almost a tradition. One of the biggest cases in recent years involved two Frenchmen, four Spanish gipsies and one woman, who between them managed to get £2 million out of the French government by registering non-existent children and claiming social security benefit. Papers were forged claiming the birth of more than 3,000 babies over a period of eight years, and two members of the consortium drew £440 a month in respect of 70 children although in reality there were no children at all.

Things have now reached the stage where employers

accept as inevitable the fact that a certain percentage of the profits will find its way into the pockets of their employees. But then few are in a position to complain, for while the man on the production line is busy syphoning off spare parts and raw materials the management is probably indulging in some even shadier activities. Cash transactions are negotiated with overseas companies, and the money deposited in a foreign bank account; claims for government subsidies for new and non-existent machinery are made and paid; the firm's accounts are fixed. But it does not even end there, for the practice continues all along the line to government level, and the only people who lose out are the honest and the weak who are effectively subsidizing everyone else.

Religion is well favoured as a front for fraudulent activity, particularly as there are no restrictions on setting up a church. People are more disposed to give their money away if they believe it to be for a religious organization, and one popular method is to persuade followers to donate a certain percentage of their income to the so-called church to further its good works.

A similar ruse was employed by two men who appeared in court in 1970 in York charged with obtaining £42,000 from a wealthy woman by telephoning her in the middle of the night and saying that the caller was God. The heavenly voice instructed her to give away large sums of money to a national charity which turned out to be rather more earthly than the woman had been led to believe.

Gullibility certainly makes life easier for the conman, but the main reason why so much fraud goes undetected is that the people who indulge in it tend to be more intelligent than the authorities who are trying to track them down. This kind of criminal is a far cry from the thug with a stocking over his face and a gun in his hand, a fact well illustrated by the recent growth of a new area of fraudulent activity, namely computers.

The advance of technology inevitably goes hand in hand with the development of more sophisticated techniques of fraud, yet the vulnerability of companies with computers is only just beginning to be realized. One of the first people to discover what was going on was Guy Parker, himself a computer expert, who one day hit on a method of moving several million dollars from the United States to Britain. Instead of doing it himself, he set out to discover how many other people were doing similar things already. In his first year of operation, during which he suggested to firms that they pay him half of any money he might save them, he made over £40,000. Significantly, as his name became known in business circles, he received as many enquiries from employees asking how to defraud their companies as he received from employers asking how to protect themselves against this kind of activity.

The main problem with computerization is that, even if it were possible for the board of directors to check every transaction going through the computer, few of them would be able to understand what they were looking at. The necessity of employing people with specialized skills puts management in a very vulnerable position *vis-à-vis* its employees, particularly as the responsibility vested in certain individuals is absolute. It is the easiest thing in the world for a processing manager or even a programmer to feed the computer false information for his own personal gain. Cheques drawn on large companies are invariably stamped as it would be impossible to sign them all by hand, and the payment of sums below a certain level is unlikely to be queried. This, together with the fact that records can easily be erased in a way that is not possible when accounts are kept in book form, means that a clever operator is unlikely to arouse suspicion. Provided that he is not too greedy and keeps the sum down to a few thousand pounds a year, the loss is likely to be written off with no questions asked.

The situation is further aggravated by the fact that, even if a computer fraud is discovered and the culprit traced, the cost to the company of taking the man to court is likely to be greater than the cost of forgetting about it altogether. 'In my experience,' says Guy Parker, 'only two such criminals have been prosecuted out of a total of more than fifty. One was sentenced to eight years in prison, the other was given five.'

The specialist undoubtedly has a head start when it comes to fraud. Anyone skilled enough to deceive the experts in his own field has a pretty good chance of deceiving the police. If the fraud is organized on a complex international basis, the chances of detection are even more remote. This tends to be the case with art forgery, which, though it requires a very high degree of skill, is one of the most lucrative areas of fraud.

Art forgery includes painting, sculpture, rare books, coins, prints, antiques and even jewellery. It covers both the reproduction of established works of art and the creation of original ones in the style of recognized artists. The fact that gifted young craftsmen can make more money by turning their talents to the production of fakes than by the exploration of their own potential is a sad reflection on the state of the art world. If art were looked upon primarily in terms of its artistic merit instead of its financial worth, this kind of forgery could not flourish in the way that it does.

Painting and sculpture are two of the most difficult items to falsify successfully, particularly now that the art market is more wary in its approach to hitherto unknown works by well-established artists. Nevertheless many forgeries do come onto the market, and many people do get fooled, from the expert who pays thousands of pounds for a forged Matisse to the simple tourist who picks up an ancient Roman figure carved only the week before.

The Italians are unusually skilled at producing classical works of art in a variety of styles, and in many cases the artist is quite unaware that his work is being passed off as genuine. The middleman is the one who makes the money, while the artist is often very poorly rewarded for his pains. Just occasionally it is possible for an exceptionally gifted man to achieve a reputation in his own right. This is what happened to Alceo Dossena, a simple stone-mason who had never had an art lesson in his life, and whose work is now valued at between one and two million dollars.

Dossena's work was exceptional, but in common with other unknown artists he did not begin to sell until he went into partnership with a shrewd middleman, in his case a goldsmith by the name of Fasoli. They met in 1916 when Fasoli bought a carved Madonna for 100 lire and was so struck by its expert craftsmanship and air of antiquity that he suggested to Dossena that it might be to their mutual advantage to go into business together. Dossena would create, Fasoli would sell.

Dossena was so delighted at the success of the arrangement and the amount of money that came pouring in (in fact it was a mere fraction of the fortune that Fasoli was making) that it never occurred to him to wonder how his work was sold or to whom. He certainly had no idea that his carvings were being passed off, sometimes with forged certificates of authenticity, as genuine antiques. Among his greatest achievements were a five and a half feet statue of Athene, heralded at the time as one of the finest examples of ancient Greek sculpture, and the famous Tomb of Savelli, described as a masterpiece of High Gothic. The Tomb was sold and resold many times before finding a home at the Boston Museum of Fine Arts, which was happy to pay 100,000 dollars for the privilege.

It was not until Dossena realized what was going on and woke up to the fact that he was the most poorly paid, that the truth began to emerge. The art world laughed at him at first, but when conclusive evidence was produced the laughter turned into an embarrassed silence. Dealers and collectors from Paris, Berlin, London and Rome were thrown into confusion by Dossena's revelations. Dossena himself died a pauper in 1937 but his work is still on show in many of the world's finest museums. Only if pressed will they admit that this or that Greek statue is in fact a forgery.

Organized art forgery today is centred mainly in Belgium, with artists and craftsmen from all over Europe contributing to this flourishing industry. With many crafts threatened by mass production and demand for craftsmen diminishing, many highly skilled men have no choice but to turn to work of this kind. It is ironical that present-day artists should have to copy the work of their predecessors in order to find a market. The paintings of Hungarian exile Elmyr de Hory only began to sell when eager collectors and dealers thought that they came from the brush of Picasso or Matisse. When they were signed de Hory no-one was interested.

It is clearly not possible to look at every aspect of fraud in a book of this length, neither is it necessary. In every fraud case someone is out to make money at someone else's expense, and the worst that can happen to the conman is that his greed will land him behind bars for a few years. Even this can sometimes be to his advantage, particularly if the hoax is outrageous enough to capture the imagination of the public. The international scandal caused by author Clifford Irving with his fake biography of millionaire Howard Hughes did more to enhance his reputation than to damage it. The story was reported in more than one newspaper as a pleasant interlude in a rather dull winter, and Irving himself, well aware of the fact that everyone loves a conman, promptly sat himself down to write a book about it.

But crime is not to everyone's taste, for a man convicted of criminal activity will carry a stigma for the rest of his life. Not that he is alone in this, for there are other ways of making money which, while not considered precisely criminal, carry the same stigma for those who choose to pursue them. In the following chapters three such individuals, a prostitute, a drug pusher and a pornographer, talk about how they make money out of the needs, obsessions and cravings of others.

Part Four

MONEY THROUGH WEAKNESS

CHAPTER SIX

Prostitution

Prostitution is alive and well and living underground. The Street Offences Act of 1959 drove it there, but even if the girls themselves are no longer allowed to walk the streets touting for trade, the signs of their existence are still clearly evident to those who know how to read between the lines. A stroll through Soho or Mayfair's Shepherd Market reveals advertising at its most subtle: private dancing lessons, new routines, all variations; large Italian chest for sale; expert tailoring, alterations done by hand; air hostess seeks interesting ground position; very strict schoolmistress has a vacancy for a wayward pupil, full equipment available—phone Miss Whiplash. Some prostitutes even advertise in the press, though newspapers are wary about what they carry. An advertisement for a photographic model, followed by her measurements, is unlikely to be accepted, whereas something as simple as 'Erection and demolition' still appears from time to time.

The refusal of newspapers to carry advertisements for prostitution is only one of the ways in which society registers its disapproval of whoring. A prostitute is treated like a leper, no longer an individual but mentally filed as a tart, fallen woman, whore, slut, harlot, and herded together with others who are no better than she. No-one says casually at dinner parties. 'Well actually, I'm a call-girl,' just as few men ever admit to having been with one. Polite society rejects the prostitute as an outcast, even if it uses her, studies her, and is insatiably curious about her.

The prostitute herself is much more honest, both about what she is and what she does. Her vision is not clouded by morality in the sense that society understands it. As far as she is concerned she is selling herself for money, no more and no less than that, for as one prostitute succinctly put it, 'All women are sitting on a fortune if only they realized it.'

To some people this is no doubt a tragedy, but the real tragedy is that even those who do realize it never make a fortune. Girls who go on the game to make money invariably spend all that they make, and when they give it up a few years later they find themselves without a penny to show for it. That is how it was with Gloria who became a prostitute when she was twenty-two and married, with two children. Now aged thirty, Gloria lives with her family in a large, rambling house in the suburbs of London, and looking at her one would never believe that she has had more men in a week than most women have in a lifetime. Her carefully made-up face, frank blue eyes and startling red hair are far from the cheap, peroxide look one has come to associate with women in her profession. But if she is attractive now, eight years ago Gloria must have been beautiful.

'I had a place at Edinburgh University when I was eighteen, and I was all set to go when I met Mike. He was fourteen years older than me and fantastically good looking, and we fell for each other just like that. If it had been London University I think I would have tried to combine the two, but Edinburgh was so far away it wasn't possible. It had to be either one or the other, so I gave up my university place and married Mike instead.

'The marriage was a disaster. We loved each other all right, but we just couldn't live with each other. Mike ran porn shops in Soho. It wasn't something he liked doing but he made a lot of money out of it. I didn't mind—I don't think it's immoral or anything like that—but what I did mind was that he never gave me any money. I always had to ask for every penny I needed. It was degrading, and when I had two kids to look after it just became ridiculous. I had a wardrobe full of evening dresses so that he could show me off in front of his friends but I didn't have a single skirt or pair of trousers to wear during the day.

'Of course he drank, and he had a never-ending stream of birds. Birds were essential to Mike, he couldn't have survived without them. I began to run away, but of course I never had any money so I always had to go back in the end. Sometimes he would come after me and beat me up—not the best way to persuade someone to come back home—but he was usually drunk when he did it anyway. In the end things got so bad I decided I couldn't stand it any more, so I picked up the kids and left.

'The first thing I had to do was get some money. I could have taken a job for about twenty quid a week, but with rent to pay, two kids to feed and someone to look after them, it wouldn't have got me very far. Besides I knew, through Mike, that decent-looking girls of about my age could make twenty quid a day, and I also had the right contacts. Well, put yourself in my position, twenty quid a week before tax or twenty quid a day tax-free, the choice seemed obvious.

'I don't regret it at all, in fact I don't even feel guilty about it. Why should I? It's my body, and if I want to sell it, flog it, or tie it up with chains that's my business. It doesn't concern anyone else. Admittedly I would never have done it if I hadn't needed the money, but having decided that going on the game was the quickest way of making it there wasn't much point in being sorry. Mike didn't give a damn when he found out later anyway. I wish in a way he had—well it would have been more normal, wouldn't it?

'I started off by calling this woman I knew in Chelsea called Jinty. She made all the arrangements and took 50% of the money, I was never paid direct. I don't think she fiddled me, but if she had I would never have known. You have to trust people when you're on the game.

'I didn't feel dirty doing it, in fact I didn't feel anything. I certainly never got any pleasure out of it, never had an orgasm or anything like that. You pretend of course, you learn to grunt and groan and moan in ecstasy, you make him think he's the greatest lover in the world, but all you're really thinking about is his money. It's a business deal, that's all.

'It's funny, people can't understand how a girl can open her legs for money, but what I don't understand is the men who come and pay for it. You get the kinks of course, the ones whose wives would have a fit if they presented them with a whip and said get on with it, but most of my clients were just ordinary businessmen. Perhaps it's safer to pay—they get the thrill of leading a double life without the danger of getting involved. Also I suppose they avoid all the bother of chatting up a girl, taking her out to dinner, making excuses to the wife. It might take a month to get her into bed, and then it might not be any good. You can get a lot of lays for the price of a month's dinners. All the same, it's rather sad. I quite liked some of them really, but I never fancied any—I couldn't have gone with them if I had.

'I had a Lord once. I'd been with Jinty about a week when she came to me and said, "Could you pretend to be a virgin?" I said you must be kidding, I've had two children! She said, "Never mind about that, just make out you're a vicar's daughter up from the country. He'll never know the difference." So I thought, well if that's what he wants to pay for, why not?

'Jinty was going to get me some red ink or cochineal or something but she got drunk and forgot about it. I got by though, I cried and moaned and threw myself around a bit—he loved it. Then I rushed off to the bathroom, hoping he'd think I'd taken the blood with me. I got fifty quid for that, which means it must have cost him a hundred, and he gave me an extra fiver on top of it so I must have played the part well. He had about thirty "virgins" after that, not one of them genuine. I still see his name in the papers now and then and I think to myself, you silly old fool, if only you knew.

'One thing you soon learn through being a prostitute is that it doesn't matter a damn whether they're Lords or bank clerks or bloody princes, they're all the same in bed. Some of them are really weird though. A friend of mine had a regular client who made her dress up in a shroud and lie in a coffin, quite still. That was the only way he could have sex with her; I suppose he was a latent necrophiliac. Anyway she got twenty-five quid each time so she didn't mind. It's all a matter of money after all.

'I had a bloke once who never even touched me. He just took me out to dinner and all I had to do was bring along as many dogs as I could get hold of. That's all he wanted, just to see me surrounded by all these dogs. I used to borrow them from my friends. They were terribly suspicious at first, they thought he was going to do something funny to their pets, but he never did. I still don't know how he got his kicks, but if you can get the money without even doing anything for it, you don't bother to ask questions.

'I suppose I made on average about 100 to 150 quid a week—imagine how much you'd have to make to get left with that after tax. Sometimes I didn't bother to work for a week or two, sometimes I even went back to Mike for a bit. There was still this kind of fatal attraction between us, but it never lasted long. He tried to blackmail me into coming back to him, saying that he'd tell my mother I was whoring. It worked for a bit because I knew she'd be horrified if she found out, but the threats became less effective after a while.

'In fact my mother came round once to see me. I had a little mews house at the time and one of the girls was there with me. My mother asked her, the way one does, what she did for a living, and this girl said, straight out, "I'm a call-girl." I nearly died, but before I could say anything my mother said brightly, "Oh, you mean a telephonist!" I didn't bother to explain.

'I did tell her myself, much later on. I don't think she really understood, but I wanted her to find out from me rather than someone else. I didn't want my father to know though, but she told him all the same. He never said anything about it, I think he convinced himself it never happened. He probably believes my kids were virgin births or something. I'm still about ten years old in his eyes.

'I stopped whoring when I was twenty-seven, partly because the kids were growing up, but mainly because I decided to leave Mike once and for all and as long as I stayed on the game I was bound to go on meeting people who knew him. Anyway I was pregnant again so it seemed a good time to give it up.

'Three months later Mike committed suicide. The vicious ones said that I killed him but it wasn't true. I think he was afraid of getting old, he was forty-one at the time and I'm sure he was scared of not being able to get the birds so easily. I sometimes think that he did it to free me, so that there could be no going back. We were still drawn to each other like magnets, right up until the end. But then perhaps I'm just imagining that so as to give myself a clear conscience, perhaps it really was my fault after all.

'The only thing I really regret about those five years is the money. It just came and went without anything to show for it. Perhaps it was because I made it so easily that I never thought twice about spending it. If I'd had to work in some stuffy office all day for a few quid I'm sure I would have had a very different attitude, but as it was I just enjoyed it. I did look good though, I looked much better when I was a prostitute than I do now. I really looked after myself. I spent more on underwear in a week than I spend now in six months. But then I was running a business I suppose, and having nice underwear was an important part of it.

'The worst thing about it was the boredom. I just stagnated mentally, almost to the point where I felt I would go out of my mind. Most prostitutes are pretty thick I suppose, so it doesn't bother them, but if you have any intelligence at all you go nuts in the end.

'I have a job now which brings in about eighty quid a month. It's not much compared with whoring, and I'd be a hypocrite if I pretended not to mind the difference in the way we live, but I wouldn't go back to it. There are some things that are right at certain times in your life and not right at others. I don't think it damaged me in any way. It didn't put me off men and it certainly didn't put me off sex. If it had any effect at all, it would show in my relationships with other people. I wouldn't know about that though, you'd have to ask them.

'I never tell anyone I was a prostitute, not because I'm ashamed of it but because their attitude changes completely as though I had some terrible disease. It's nobody's business anyway, why should I justify my life to anyone?

'The kids don't know anything about it, they don't even know what their father did. I don't think I could tell them either, but I wouldn't lie to them if they asked. It's nothing to do with them really.

'If my daughter wants to be a prostitute when she grows up, I won't try and stop her. It's her body and she has the right to do what she likes with it. I hope she doesn't though. I don't know why, I just think there are better ways of making money.'

And so there are. But there are worse ways as well, and one of them is drugs. Unlike prostitution, which is a gentlewoman's pastime by comparison, the drug scene is cruel, vicious, and frequently lethal. But for those, like Bobby, who manage to survive, there is more money to be made out of this particular obsession in a week or two than most people can hope to make in a whole year.

CHAPTER SEVEN

Drugs

In Manila, capital of the Philippines, drug pushers run the risk of being murdered by privately hired assassins. Wealthy families, anxious to protect their children from exploitation, readily pay between $600 and $1,000 a time to have suspects eliminated, reasoning that if they do not kill the pushers then the drugs will kill their children.

In London pushers are luckier. The Misuse of Drugs Act, passed in July 1971, lays down a maximum penalty of fourteen years imprisonment and/or a fine. By British standards this is a fairly heavy sentence for a non-violent crime, yet many people, while having no wish to degenerate into anything approaching the situation in Manila, are of the opinion that it is still grossly inadequate. Drugs, after all, can kill and the number of people addicted to dangerous drugs such as heroin and LSD is on the increase.

Certainly the drug business is still very much in evidence in the traditional areas of London, like Piccadilly and the back streets of Soho. Everything is available at a price—heroin, cocaine, acid, amphetamines, barbiturates, cannabis—and competition among pushers is strong and sometimes violent. Not long ago, in the early hours of the morning, Bobby was stabbed in the stomach by a rival operator and ended up in hospital with a ruptured spleen. It might have made him change his mind about selling drugs but it did not. Instead, with a two inch scar across his stomach, Bobby simply moved his pitch from Piccadilly to the comparative safety of the Elephant and Castle.

Bobby is a junkie as well as a pusher. Addicted to heroin and barbiturates, he takes any drugs he can lay his hands on—cocaine, acid, amphetamines, cannabis, morphine, physeptone, opium, methedrine. 'It's beautiful man, just beautiful. When you get the buzz there's nothing like it.' He is twenty-two, though he says with a grin that he feels about sixty, and he has been taking heroin since he was fifteen. He frequently expresses genuine surprise at the fact that he is still alive.

At first sight Bobby certainly looks healthy enough, and he is even attractive in his own way. Dressed in cotton jeans and a bush jacket he brings to mind a taller and younger version of the Maharishi, with long black hair curling over his shoulders, thick moustache and beard, and a thin string of coloured beads hanging round his neck. There are none of the obvious signs of decay normally associated with drug-addiction—emaciation, pallor, fatigue. But on closer examination one notices that his tattooed hands, badly stained with nicotine, shake uncontrollably as he lights one (straight) cigarette after the other; his green eyes are slightly clouded, their pupils over-large, and he is continually scratching his stomach through his thin, blue tee shirt (an effect, he says apologetically, of the heroin). So far Bobby has spent three and a half of his twenty-two years either in borstal or in a prison cell. His last sentence ended only a few months ago and already he faces another conviction for conspiring to sell drugs. He has been pushing drugs since he was nineteen and in spite of what he has been through he has not the slightest intention of giving it up.

'I was brought up in the East End of London by my mother, who was an American Indian, and a succession of so-called "stepfathers" who stayed for a while and then pissed off. My real father died when I was two. He was Irish, that's about all I know.

'I don't remember all that much about my childhood—the psychos say that's because I've blotted it out of my mind—but I do remember that we were always very poor. My mother never worked and we depended on these blokes who came and went from time to time. One of them was a long-distance lorry driver and he was well paid—about forty or fifty quid a week I think. Not only that but he was a thief as well. He would pile an extra three piece suite onto the lorry and flog it for himself somewhere along the line, you know the sort of thing. We were okay while he was with us but unfortunately he didn't stay very long.

'I left school when I was fifteen and went into the merchant navy. Perhaps I needed to get away; I don't know, I never try and look at reasons for things. Anyway it was then, on a trip to Morocco, that I was first offered heroin, and being curious like any other kid, I tried it. At that time I was so green I hadn't the slightest idea what the stuff was, let alone that it was addictive or dangerous. I just tried it, liked it and began taking it regularly. Not fixing you understand—I didn't have the courage to use a hypodermic for a long time—just sniffing it the way one takes snuff. Within a few months, without even realizing it, I was a heroin addict.

'I can't describe what it's like, it's just fantastic, beautiful. I know I've been lucky, no-one can understand why it hasn't killed me yet and I know that if I don't get off it soon then it will kill me. That's the trouble with this game—most of my friends are dead already.

'Anyway I stayed in the merchant navy for a year and

then, when I was sixteen, I went to work as a porter at King's College Hospital. It wasn't easy for me to get heroin then, me being only a kid and the pushers round Piccadilly all being men, so I started filling up with morphine instead. A nurse at the hospital used to get it for me. What she did was give the patient only half the dose prescribed by the doctor, fill it up with water, and slip me the other half. Usually the patient couldn't tell the difference anyway, but I still feel bad about it even now. The nurse is dead now. She was a junkie too.

'I hadn't been at the hospital very long before my mother was taken ill. She had been on sleeping pills for as long as I could remember and she had become addicted. It's funny, you'd think it would have put me off, seeing what the barbiturates did to her, but it didn't. She used to have fits, even convulsions, quite without warning, just like I do now when the barbs wear off. The authorities took me into a home, saying that I was too young to cope with all the responsibility of cleaning and cooking and looking after my mother and two younger sisters as well. I've never forgiven them for that. I didn't mind doing it a bit, the house was tiny and anyway she was my mother, I loved her.

'To make me go quietly they promised they would get someone to come in every day to see to her and to clean the place up. Like hell they did! When she died soon afterwards her body lay on the floor for a whole week before anyone came near the place. Then, to make it even worse, two weeks later a letter arrived offering us a council house. We'd been on the waiting list for fifteen years and never heard a bloody word in all that time. That's really sick, you can't get much sicker than that.

'After my mother died I really started fixing like crazy,

not just heroin but anything I could get hold of. I ran away from the home together with a friend and we wound up on a farm where we got a job picking fruit. We were both into drugs about as far as you can get and one night, stoned out of our minds, we stole several crates of fruit from a stationary lorry. We didn't want the stuff, it was for kicks, we didn't even know what we were doing. You won't believe it but we got landed with twenty-two months in borstal for that. Twenty-two months! People get less than that for physical assault. But of course it wasn't really the offence, it was the fact that we were junkies that did it. The law hates us, it makes sure we always come off worse than everyone else.

'I was put in prison while they decided which borstal I was to go to, and there, for the first time, I had no drugs and no means of getting any from outside. That was when I did my first Cold Turkey (that's what we call withdrawals). The screws just threw me in a padded cell, locked the door and left me to get on with it, the same as they do with all addicts. I've been through Cold Turkey three times since then but it doesn't get any better. Your eyes run, your nose runs, you vomit, get uncontrollable muscle spasms, severe stomach cramps and permanent diarrhoea. It can last days, sometimes weeks, but however long it lasts it's sheer bloody hell. You really think you're going to die. I've done it twice in prison and each time they locked the door and left me there, without even a toilet, just a pot. When they looked in five days later the cell was just revolting with shit and vomit all over the floor—I'm sorry but that's how it was. Two other junkies did die while I was in there. It happens so easily because when you get these stomach cramps you can't even move, you just have to lie there on your back and wait for it to pass. If you vomit at the same time you've had it. That's what happened to the other two, they were asphyxiated, but as far as I'm concerned they were murdered by the prison authorities.

'By the time I got out of borstal I was nineteen and the price of heroin had gone up from 17 pence to £1.25 a pill —that's one sixth of a grain. Since I had no money, no home and no job I collected social security and started pushing, it seemed the obvious thing to do. Of course I went back to drugs myself, even though I wasn't physically dependent on them any more by then. It's the mental withdrawal that's the hardest part; doctors say it takes about five years to come off completely. I'm trying to get off heroin now but it's hard, particularly when you're right into the drug scene like I am.

'I don't push heroin though, anything else but not heroin. It's okay for me, I can handle it, but I wouldn't want to be responsible for supplying it to others. I've seen too much of what it can do to people, and anyway English heroin is hardly available any more. All you get now is the Chinese stuff which is impure and dangerous to fix, not only because of the impurities but because you can't tell how strong it is and so it's easy to overdose. Mostly I push acid, cannabis and speed, and I like to think that I sell to people who know what they're doing. Of course in this game you can never be sure and I did once sell some acid to a guy who jumped out of a window during his trip because he thought he was a bird. Luckily it was a first floor window and he only broke his ankle, but it could just as easily have been the seventh.

'One thing I do know for sure and that is that I never sell rubbish. Anyone who scores off me knows that he's getting first rate dope at a fair price, not like these shits in Piccadilly who charge the earth for bits of black crayon and other rubbish which is supposed to be acid. Perhaps it's because I'm a junkie myself and I know what it's like to be taken on. I may be doing something illegal but at least I can say that I do it honestly.

'Of course the stuff passes through God knows how many hands before it gets to the pusher in the street. Each one takes his own cut, both in money and in dope, but it's the guy at the top who really makes it big. He's the one riding around in a Rolls Royce and smoking a fat cigar. My eight hundred quid a week is peanuts compared to what he makes out of it. Of course I could make many times that amount if I were to sell crap like most people do, but as I said before I won't do that. I like the stuff too much myself.

'To give you an idea of how it works, I get the stuff from several one-man contacts who each supply me with their own particular drug at an agreed price. At the moment I'm paying £16 for a hundred tabs of acid, £90 to £100 for a pound weight of Pakistani black, and around £5 or £6 for a hundred tabs of speed. Speed is cheaper because a lot of it is made by bent chemical manufacturers who can't be too fussy about what they charge. Anyway I then pass the stuff on to other junkies, mostly in certain pubs, sometimes in a private house. I shared a house with some mates of mine until I went back to prison, and while I was there we had between 30 and 40 people a day coming to score off us. My own selling prices are a straight 50 pence for a tab of acid, no matter how strong it is, whether it's pink microdot, Californian sunshine, strawberry fields, white light, purple A's; £120 to £140 for a pound of best cannabis and something like 10 pence for a tab of speed. So I suppose my own profit on the deal is about £35 on the acid, £5 or so on the speed and £40 to £50 on every pound of cannabis. Like I said it comes out at around £800 a week which isn't much considering that I have to use £500 of it to buy more supplies.

'I don't think I'm doing anything immoral. I'm not fucking anyone's life up or anything. I sell to people I know and who I know can handle the stuff. Anyway they'd only buy it from someone else if they didn't get it from me and they'd probably get a far worse deal into the bargain. It's not that the money's important to me—I'm a socialist and if I could think of some way to live without it I would—but you need money in this system, you can't live without it, and let's face it, pushing is better than working.

'Not that I haven't worked in the past; I have, and I've paid my tax like everyone else. That's why I take social security, after all if the state thinks I have a right to it then who the hell am I to argue? I certainly don't need the money but I take it as a protest, a protest against the system. I hate the bloody system. It's there for the good of the blokes at the top, that's all.

'I would never steal anything though, or do anything violent. I'm a pacifist, I hate violence. I did once shoplift to get some bread to buy heroin when I was desperate. I don't think that was right either, stealing is never right, but after all they were only capitalists, those shopkeepers, making money out of the working classes. I wouldn't do it again but I don't have a conscience about it, it doesn't keep me awake at night.

'I'm glad I was born into a working-class family. I'd hate to be part of the middle classes, living in a semi in the suburbs and working from nine to five every day. I know someone's got to do it, but it's just not my scene. Nor is being rich, I would hate that even more, I'm sure it's wrong to be able to ride around in a flashy car, even if you've worked hard for it all your life. It must be wrong when so many people have nothing at all.

'I suppose I don't really have any feeling for money, for what it can buy. All I need it for is to be free and to get my drugs. Apart from that most of it goes on cigarettes, about 60 a day at the moment. That's what's going to get me in the end, cancer not heroin. I like having a lot of money though. It's another way of showing the system that I can manage very well without it.

'I think perhaps I would work if I had responsibility, if I settled down to live with a chick and we had a kid. I already have a kid in fact, a boy eighteen months old. He lives in Austria with his mother who is Viennese. She was deported for possessing cannabis, though, to tell you the truth, she was covering for me at the time. I see them as often as I can, the fare's not that much even by air. I love my kid, I really do, even though he was an accident. I never loved his mother though, we just went together, you know how it is. The funny part is that her old man's a psychiatrist of all things.

'I really don't know what I want to do with my life. I never make plans, just live for today and take tomorrow as it comes. What's the point of making plans two weeks in advance anyway? I might be dead by then. I suppose all I really want is for people to leave me alone.'

As long as he sticks to his present occupation of drug-pushing, however, Bobby is not likely to be left alone for very long. It is for this reason that this shady activity does not suit everyone, for in spite of the rewards it may have to offer, some people still prefer to sleep soundly in their beds at night. In any case there are plenty of other ways of making money, ways which are just as lucrative and far less alarming. One of the oldest and most successful money-spinners of all time is pornography.

CHAPTER EIGHT

Pornography

In a backstreet office block just a few steps away from one of Copenhagen's main shopping areas Henrik Moeller, Denmark's King of the 8 mm porno film, is making a movie. As the camera moves in for a copulation close-up, ensuring that the models' private parts will soon become public knowledge, Henrik stretches out beneath his favourite photograph of Lord Longford and stifles a yawn. This is his third film this week and he is tired.

It is 9.30 p.m., three hours since they began working on the movie's hard-core sequences and a good twelve hours since the beginning of the day's work. Soon it will be finished and just as well, for the actors are beginning to tire too. Not all of them can sleep tomorrow; some must study and others have to be up early to see to their families. Pornography, after all, is simply a part-time job to bring in some extra money.

For Henrik, however, pornography is a business and a very lucrative business at that. It brought him in well over £50,000 profit last year from blue films alone, and including his book and magazine interests the total was considerably higher. Thanks to pornography Henrik Moeller, still in his early thirties, is a rich man.

By 10.00 p.m. the last model has plodded wearily down the rickety wooden staircase to the street and Henrik is left alone with an assortment of frilly underwear, high-heeled boots and shoes and a comprehensive selection of sexual equipment. He lops the top off a new bottle of beer, settles back in his favourite Arne Jacobsen easy chair, and like any other businessman at the end of a day, starts talking about his work.

'I began making pornographic movies about six years ago when I was 27. I was fed up with my job and I wanted to make some money, real money, not just enough to scrape by. I chose pornography because, at the time, it seemed the best way to get what I wanted, but even so I must say that I never expected it to be quite the success it has turned out to be. To give you an idea of what I mean, I suppose I am now making about 100 films a year at a cost of between £550 and £850 each. I sell these films to the porno shops for £2 a copy (which isn't much considering that they then retail them for £8 or so), but even at that competitive price I still reckon on getting my money back and making at least 80% clear profit on each film.

'I must admit that I've been lucky though, because my success has largely been due to other people's failure. When I first came into the business six years ago there were lots of film companies turning out different kinds of 8 mm pornography, but now there are none left to speak of. The demand for blue films is not as great as it was and so all the inefficient or amateur companies that sprang up in the early days have fizzled out. If my own sales have increased it is only because others have gone out of business, and the way things are now it looks as though I shall very soon be the only one left. I suppose I could theoretically name any price I liked when that happens but I don't think I will because the higher sales make up for the lower profit margins anyway.

'The main reason why I have succeeded, I think, is simply professionalism. Pornography is a business like any other business and if it is to make maximum profits it must be efficiently run and properly organized. This means, for instance, that I have the latest photographic equipment available on the market and I do all my own developing and printing to keep down costs. I don't play about with any mail order exporting; it isn't worth it, and I don't have anything to do with any of the live sex shows in town either. This has nothing to do with morals or anything like that, it simply isn't good business sense. An investment like that can only work if one is able to be there the whole time watching over everything, otherwise half the takings vanish at source.

'The most important single element in making a successful pornographic movie has got to be the models. Most of mine come to me through advertisements, but some come along because they've heard of us or because friends have given them our name. A good reputation is important if you want to attract the right kind of people.

'I must say I have never had any trouble in finding models. On the contrary, every advertisement always produces more people than I can use. All kinds of people come looking for jobs, housewives, secretaries, students. The oldest one at the moment is a man of 65 and the youngest is a 15-year-old girl. The legal age limit in Denmark is 18, but I don't care about that; the girl in question is mature enough to know what she is doing and if she's willing and able to do what is required I see no reason for refusing her a job. I would never use children, though, either in films or magazines. A few people do, I know, but I don't want anything to do with it. It's not only wrong, it's dangerous.

'I'm very careful about who I take on, in fact. I certainly wouldn't take everyone who applied, even if I were in a position to do so. I don't think it's enough just to have the obvious requirements of lack of shyness, a good face and figure, and the ability to relax in front of a camera. As far as I'm concerned that's only the beginning. All would-be models are carefully processed before we decide whether to take them on or not. This means going into all aspects of their private lives, checking on their motives and backgrounds so that we don't find ourselves with people who are mentally unbalanced or sexually abnormal. It also means that we keep files on everybody we do accept, so that we have a permanent index of all the things that people are prepared to do and anything they refuse to do, such as perversions of some kind. It's also useful to have a record of any natural tendencies towards sadism or masochism, so that when scenes of this kind are needed models can be used in a way that corresponds with their natural preferences. I would never try to make anyone do anything he or she didn't want to do.

'One thing that all models have in common of course, is the wish to make some extra money. The girls get £40 for an assignment, regardless of the length of time they have been with us or the time it takes to complete the shooting. Most films are finished in a day or two, but the fee remains the same however long it takes. Men are paid slightly more, about £55, because their part is more difficult. After all, it's obvious if a man is interested or not but a girl can easily pretend without anyone being any the wiser.

'If models are particularly good then they are rewarded by the fact that we use them more often. I never discriminate by paying anyone more than anyone else. There are film producers who pay their models according to how sexy they are or how good or bad their performance has been that day, but I don't believe in doing that. I think it's unfair and it's also very unwise because potentially good models won't come back a second time. In any case performance is something that can never be guaranteed in this type of film. If a man has trouble getting an erection, for instance, which is something that happens quite often, we all just sit around and have a drink and a chat until he is able to carry on. I wouldn't think of paying him any less, after all it happens to all of us at some time or other.

'Honesty is something that I feel very strongly about. I always tell the models who apply for jobs exactly what is required of them and make sure that they realize that the films will be freely available in the shops afterwards. I have heard of people who try and make out that they deal with overseas buyers only and that the film will never be seen anywhere in Denmark. In fact, from my own experience, I would say that there is very little social stigma attached to this kind of work and in many cases girls even discuss it with their families beforehand.

'Another sign of respectability if you like is that we quite often get married or engaged couples who need to make a lot of money quickly or who are saving up for something like a car or a holiday. Past experience has taught me never to use them in the same scene though, because when there is group sex or something like that then they both start looking out of the corner of their eye to see what the other one is up to. If I use them separately, at different times or on different days, then they don't get jealous.

'This might sound silly, but it is in fact very important

because none of my models can afford to be motivated by emotion of any kind. This is a business and it is important for me to have models who approach it in a business-like way. After all, they are being paid to do a job and that job is to do what the director wants them to do, not what they feel like doing themselves.

'Shooting is obviously made a lot easier by the fact that there is no soundtrack, but there is always a story of some kind. I'm sure that this is important because without a story people cannot identify with what is going on and the whole purpose of the film is lost. The theme must be simple for the same reason—for instance a man sees a girl on a beach and invites her for a drink, a girl hitch-hiker thumbs a lift from two men in a van. If there is no story at all then the film can only be bad because it is not enough just to see people fucking. The viewer must know the circumstances that led up to the fucking if he is to become involved. I'm not saying that my films are artistic, they're not. After all, I'm not trying to compete with MGM or United Artists. If people want to see a polished and professional product they know where to find it, and it's not in the porn shops. People who buy pornography want to see sex, not art, and sex is what I set out to provide.

'I really don't know what makes a successful blue film though, I wish I did. I have compared the ones that sell well with the ones that sell badly to see if I can find a pattern of some kind, but there seems to be no common denominator at all. About 90% of my films show straightforward couple or group sex, including lesbian and homosexual acts, because that is what most people want to see. The rest show perversions of some kind, flagellation and animal sex, things like that, but that is really specialist material and there is not all that much demand for it. People who are hooked on these things usually do them in their private lives anyway.

'Most of our customers are obviously tourists, with the Japanese, Germans and British taking the largest share of the market. The Danes buy relatively little pornography, and I'm sure that if other countries were to allow the same freedom that we have here then the industry would die in a very short time. What happened over here was that demand soared dramatically for about the first six months after censorship was lifted, and then it began to fall off. It's surprising how quickly one gets used to looking at pornography, and when it's no longer forbidden most people seem to feel that when you've seen one blue film you've seen them all. Not everyone thinks that way of course, and we regularly get letters from Danish people asking us to do more and more hard-core pornography. As long as there is enough demand I shall be happy to go on satisfying it.

'People sometimes ask me if being in this business has put me off sex in my private life, but quite honestly the two things have nothing to do with each other. As far as I'm concerned what goes on in front of the camera is of professional interest only, it neither excites me nor bores me. The models are my employees and after all it's no fun if you can tell a girl to take her clothes off and do anything you want her to do. Where's the excitement in that? I must admit that I felt a bit strange at first telling them to do these things, but I soon got used to it, particularly as they never refused. When I'm on my own though, and I see an attractive girl walking down the street, I react in just the same way as any other man would. After all, it's the mystery that makes sex exciting.

'In case you're wondering about that photograph, by the way, I put it there because I really like Lord Longford. When he left Denmark the newspapers said that in spite of everything he was turned on a little by what he saw here. I was really pleased about that—pornography doesn't turn me on at all.'

It seems that Henrik Moeller is not the only one to have a soft spot for Lord Longford, for while censorship laws make sure that the Danish pornographers stay in business they also provide the necessary background for a flourishing industry in Britain. There are of course no official statistics but unofficial information from people who are in the know indicates that the selling of hard-core pornography in this country is at the very least a £10 million a year business. If soft-core material such as full frontal nude pin-ups and so-called sex instruction books and films is included, then the figure leaps to a total of several hundred million pounds a year.

The profits are truly staggering. In Soho, for instance, a 200 foot colour film of the type that Henrik produces sells under the counter for £30 while a similar film in black and white can be bought for £15. Books and magazines that are available in Copenhagen for less than £1 retail in London for between £4 and £6 each. With prices like that it is hardly surprising that profits in any one of Soho's flourishing porn shops can average something in the region of £1,000 a week. The total annual turnover of these shops is estimated to be at least £3 million. It is not only the owners who make fast money either. A shop manager can easily earn £100 a week, and his assistants can expect to take home £40 to £50 each in return for a few hours of part-time work. The rates are high because it is likely to be the front man who carries the risk of prosecution and not the real owner. Once a man is convicted he is no longer of any use to the trade.

While much of the material on sale in porn shops is of Scandinavian origin, nevertheless a good deal of it is produced in Britain. Since there is no law against filming pornographic material in private but only against distributing it, a handful of photographers are prepared to undertake this kind of assignment in return for a suitably large fee. One London photographer is regularly rewarded with £250 for an 8 mm home movie completed in a day. Such films are usually sent abroad for developing and printing and then often re-imported as foreign products.

In view of the delicate legal position it is very much more difficult to get models in Britain than it is in Scandinavia. Explicit advertising is out of the question and the photographer has to rely on personal contacts or word of mouth introductions. Many of the models are housewives, students and would-be starlets who, like their Scandinavian counterparts, are anxious to make some extra money. For a two- to three-hour photographic session they can expect to earn between £25 and £30. Since models are scarce there is no question of inquiring into their motives or probing the details of their private lives. Anyone who is reasonably attractive and able to perform in front of a camera is bound to be accepted on the spot.

Blue films, photographs and magazines are not available only in the porn shops; they also form the basis for a flourishing mail order business. Many operators are based overseas, attracting tourists with direct advertisements in shop windows, but there are also about seventy mail order firms within the U.K. reaping a total turnover of at least £4 million a year. Most of the businesses are run by one man with a mailing list of some 1,000 names, but a handful are really big, supplying material to between 5,000 and 15,000 people. Mail order pornography is cheaper than pornography under the counter, with films priced £3 to £5 lower than in the shops. Customers are tempted to buy by tantalizing titbits usually displayed on film boxes. This is one of the milder ones:

'Leo is really surprised when his new girlfriend starts tearing off his clothes and ties him up, whipping and biting him. All this is happening in unbelievable excitement.'

The exorbitant prices that these films can command are justified by the distributors on the grounds that pornography is not generally available. Thanks to the censorship laws, purveyors of porn are easily able to charge four, six, even eight times the value of the product, knowing that whatever they charge people will always be prepared to buy. The rich rewards of the underground sex industry guarantee that it will never die out, just as the fact that pornography is forbidden guarantees that there will always be a market for it. None of the people who are now lining their pockets through pornography want to see a change in the law. They know full well that if freedom were to replace censorship, the profits of sin would slump in a very short time. One organ, after all, is pretty much like another.

And so, while the battle rages between moralists and reformers, the pornographers continue to prosper and grow rich. The banning of pornography has resulted in a flourishing black market, not unlike the illegal abortion racket. In fact the pornography debate and the abortion debate have much in common. Pornographers, however, are motivated solely by money, whereas some abortionists at least are inspired by higher ideals as well. In the next chapter a London abortionist explains why, for him, money is not enough.

CHAPTER NINE

Abortion

In spite of the fact that abortion has been performed for centuries, the idea of ending a pregnancy still meets with more hysterical reaction than rational comment. Abortion remains a loaded word and abortionist even more so. The public image of the abortionist is either that of a profit-hungry medical practitioner trading on human misery or, even worse, an unqualified quack wielding unspeakable instruments while a poor girl cowers in a corner clutching a fistful of borrowed notes. Both these pictures are exaggerations, but fact is so clouded by fantasy and hypocrisy that anyone concerned with abortion is automatically suspect.

The Abortion Act of 1967 aroused much controversy and concentrated a great deal more attention on the subject than it had ever received before. Suddenly everyone had something to say about it—churchmen, politicians, doctors, journalists—but the end result was that, instead of being dispersed, the clouds of fantasy and hypocrisy were thickened.

A good few years after the passing of the Act, the subject of abortion is as explosive as ever. Figures are still based on conjecture rather than fact, and the view most often quoted is still that of the extremist. The anti-abortionists have the loudest and most organized voices so they are the ones most frequently heard, but they must know, even as they raise their voices and clamour for a change in the law, that abortion can never be stopped. As long as there is sex there will be unwanted pregnancy and as long as there is unwanted pregnancy there will be abortion. The politicians, moralists, churchmen and doctors who campaign for abortion to be made more difficult are underestimating the persistence of desperate women. The qualified abortionist who is maligned for trading on human misery is surely more humanitarian than the dedicated doctor who drives his patient into the arms of a back-street quack.

It is indicative of the general hysteria surrounding the subject that doctors who perform abortions for fee-paying patients are treated far less kindly than doctors who operate under the National Health Service. The fact of money changing hands seems to make it too disgusting to contemplate, while women who are able to find the means to pay are generally regarded as being beyond sympathy. It is as though abortion becomes more acceptable if the doctors do not make so much money and the women are seen to be helpless.

Curiously enough the views of those directly involved in abortion are heard far less than others. Women who have had abortions are sometimes encouraged to write letters to the press, but patients are talked about much more than they are talked to. The same is true of the doctors who perform the operations and while some of them may be concerned about the possibility of attracting adverse publicity that is not the main reason for their silence. The truth of the matter is that they have little or nothing to gain by speaking out, but they do have a great deal to lose. Adding fuel to the fire of the abortion debate only results in increased publicity and makes their job even more difficult. The best way for a doctor to further the cause of abortion is not to present his side of the argument but to keep quiet and get on with doing it. And that is exactly what Doctor B does.

Doctor B has a well-established private practice in central London. He is approaching middle-age, married with two teenage girls, and has a kindly and unhurried manner. About two-thirds of his professional time is taken up with matters of abortion and contraception, and he has very little patience with those who oppose his work, particularly those within his own profession.

'Doctors who say that abortion is unpleasant are simply being ridiculous. Clearing someone's bowels manually is unpleasant, removing a six-week-old sanitary towel is unpleasant, but there is certainly nothing unpleasant about abortion. In any case medicine is full of distasteful things, and any doctor who is incapable of dissociating himself emotionally from what he has to do should not be a doctor in the first place. As for the nurses who complain about how the operation affects them, most of them have had it done themselves at some time or other. People are such hypocrites when it comes to abortion—there's a world of difference between what they say in public and what they do in private.

'My first abortion in 1948 was performed on a nurse. In fact it was mainly due to nurses and hospital secretaries that the practice snowballed. At one time I could hardly get into my own surgery because of the crowds of nurses waiting outside. All of them were done for nothing of course, but when they started sending their friends as well it got so out of hand that I had to try and do something about it. Once you start doing abortion though, it's virtually impossible to stop. People soon get to hear about it and they won't let you stop. I never actually decided to become an abortionist, my practice just grew out of the demand for it.

'In my own experience doctors who specialize in abortion tend to be kind people with a soft spot for women. This is particularly true of the older ones who were really taking risks when they decided to help girls in trouble. It's fatuous to suggest that abortionists trade on human misery. What does a plastic surgeon trade on, or a heart specialist? Medicine is based on misery, with the exception of planned childbirth, and the important thing for a doctor is not the cause but the effect. It's the end product, providing relief, that matters and this applies to abortion as much as to anything else. In fact it probably applies more to abortion, because when I think of the thousand or so tonsils that I've removed over the years, I'm sure that at least half of them could well have stayed where they were.

'I charge from nothing to £120 for an abortion. A lot depends on the clinic, prices vary from place to place, but I myself never see more than £20 of it. The rest goes to cover the cost of the bed, the anaesthetist, the operating theatre. Of course different doctors have different charges, and the most I've ever known anyone charge for a straightforward private abortion is £200. A more complicated abdominal operation is more expensive, maybe as much as £400 or £500.

'I suppose I spend about an hour a day actually operating, from which I get about £500 or £600 a week. Against that I have a surgery to pay for, a chauffeur-driven car to fetch people from the station when they arrive in London and of course I have to pay tax. My practice is strictly legal because in this business it's not worth being anything else. I operate in legal clinics, declare every operation and pay whatever income tax is due. With the Inland Revenue it's best to play straight because if they get suspicious they never leave you alone. Not everyone takes that view though, which is why no-one knows for sure how many abortions are done in the course of a year. The undeclared ones and the back-street ones are a completely unknown quantity.

'I used to do a lot of operations for nothing, as I mentioned before, but I do far fewer now. Apart from the odd exception I don't believe that people really appreciate what they don't pay for nowadays. It's the outcome of the Welfare State—you give people more and more and instead of saying thank you they say it's not enough. In any case it's just hypocrisy to pretend that National Health Service doctors provide their services for nothing. No-one works for nothing. They are simply paid by other people, by the hospital or the government. I have no part in the National Health Service and my practice is therefore my only source of income. When I do an operation for nothing, it really is for nothing.

'The people who seem to think that there is something criminal about charging for abortions are simply not worth arguing with. If you see something you want in a shop window you expect to have to pay for it. No-one gives me anything for nothing, I can't write to the Electricity Board and say that I have been doing half my operations for nothing so could they please cut my electricity bill. Besides, no-one is forced to come to me, no-one is forced to pay me a penny. My patients come of their own free will and either accept my charges or decide to go elsewhere.

'If Engelbert Humperdinck were to announce that he made a million pounds last year, people would just say, "Cor, lucky bloke, I wish I were him", but if I were to stand up and say that I made £500 last week from doing abortions everyone would think that was terrible. Yet what contribution does a pop singer make to society, where are his years of training and education? It doesn't even begin to make sense.

'Organized opposition to abortion has increased since the 1967 Act because of the publicity given to it. Before the Act was passed no-one talked about it very much but doctors who were prepared to do abortions knew one another well—it was like a small club. Any one of them would rush half way across London at a moment's notice to help a colleague in trouble. Now the situation has changed because as more and more doctors have come in, mutual support has been replaced by competition. A doctor in trouble can no longer call on his colleagues for help because now a doctor in trouble simply means more business for his rivals. The older ones will still come if necessary but the young ones don't have that attitude. It was the spirit of revolution that united doctors before the Act.

'As far as I'm concerned, abortion is no different from any other medical operation. I would like to know where people who talk about the sanctity of human life get their argument from, because there is certainly nothing to that effect to be found in the Bible. I had a very thorough religious upbringing and I can assure you that neither the Old nor the New Testament contains anything to suggest that human life is sacred. Any so-called sanctity is man-made and artificial, and so is the guilt and shame often attributed to girls who have had abortions. I have had everyone through here, secretaries, teachers and nuns, not to mention half the daughters of the House of Commons and even H.R.Hs. If any of them felt guilty it was because society or the people they had gone to for help had made them feel that way. Certainly none of them ever regretted the abortion afterwards.

'If I really wanted to exploit people I would do what the so-called élite of the medical profession do and charge £300 or £400 for a simple tonsil operation. These doctors are the same ones who stand up and declare that abortion is getting out of hand. There is so much professional jealousy that the real issues get clouded over.

'Ironically enough the ones who do the most damage are the churchmen and politicians who carry on about abortion being sinful while their own daughters are forced to get themselves aborted in secret. I know at once that any girl whose father is anything to do with the church will not want him to know anything about it. She is scared stiff of being thrown out of the house or of bringing shame on her parents—that's Christianity for you.

'But the hypocrisy doesn't even end there. I've operated on several girls who were actually made pregnant by Catholic priests, more often than not as the result of a regular relationship. One of them was a nun and another girl is now on the pill, but because her lover is an American priest she only sees him for about three months out of every twelve when he comes to Europe. It may surprise you but I've had quite a few nuns come to me for abortions. One even came all the way from Rome to get help, she was so desperate. Being nuns they are understandably more embarrassed and more upset than other women but after they've had their abortion they still go back to their previous life as though nothing had happened. I must admit I find that particularly hard to understand, even being in this profession where things are rarely what they seem anyway.

'There is no doubt, however, that people *are* confused

about abortion and the main reason for that is that far too much notice is taken of people with titles, whether they are archbishops, professors, lords or under-secretaries of state. The fact that they have a title gives immediate authority to their views and causes untold damage. People automatically assume that Sir someone-or-other must know what he's talking about, whereas what he is saying could well be absolute rubbish. The fact that someone has taken a few more examinations, read a few more books and acquired a few more letters after his name does not make him a better human being or give him any greater understanding of life than someone else who has not done these things. I don't stand in awe of people in authority, whoever they are, Prime Minister, Archbishop of Canterbury or Prince Philip. As far as I'm concerned they are all men with two testicles, a penis and fillings in their teeth. You can't see what I've seen in life and still be impressed by appearances.

'I'm not trying to pretend that abortionists are perfect by any means. It's quite true that some of them make a lot of money by attracting foreign business, just as it's true that others make even more money by fiddling their accounts. But let's keep it in proportion—the majority never get into the newspapers. They are simply doing what any private doctor does, providing a service and charging according to its worth. I firmly believe that my fee is a fair one, not only because I know what I'm doing but because it includes advice on contraception after the operation. I don't want to see a girl back in my surgery a couple of months later because she's pregnant again. My aim is to give long-term help, otherwise there's no point.

'The back-street boys of course don't care about anything other than the immediate situation. It's difficult to be sure because no-one knows the facts, but I don't think that back-street abortions have been affected very much by the 1967 Act. The London ones still have contacts planted in hotels and restaurants waiting to hear of someone in trouble so that they can pass on the necessary telephone number or address. Some of the back-street abortionists are quite competent, though God knows there is enough of a risk performing any operation under ideal conditions without increasing the risk by doing it on a sofa in a back room somewhere.

'The only direct involvement I ever had with an illegal case started when an Italian girl came to me from a hotel in Earls Court where she was working. Her period was late and she wanted to know if she was pregnant. Since she was only about a week overdue, I explained that it was too early to tell, gave her some pills to bring on the bleeding and told her that if nothing happened she was to come back again in about two weeks' time.

'Four or five weeks went by and I heard nothing of her, so I assumed that she must have been all right. Then one evening the telephone rang and it was the police asking if I had seen a Miss So-and-So recently as they had found an appointment card in her handbag. I looked up my files and it was this same girl. Apparently what had happened was that she had been told by someone in the hotel to go and see this old man who would get her out of trouble. Foolishly she went, not even knowing for certain whether or not she was pregnant, and a few hours later she was in hospital having her womb removed.

'The policewoman who went round to the abortionist's place said that it was like something out of a horror film—layers of dust six inches thick and terrifying instruments that looked as though they hadn't been washed in 35 years.

She said she didn't know how any girl could possibly have stayed there, it was so appalling. He didn't even check to see whether she was pregnant before he went ahead, just ruptured her womb and turned her out into the street to bleed. That is the kind of thing the anti-abortionists are helping to promote.

'If one of my daughters ever became pregnant I would have no hesitation in having her aborted. What on earth does a 19-year-old girl want with a child? I've seen real misery with girls who have either decided or been forced to go through with their pregnancies. That's where the real suffering lies, not with abortion.'

Be that as it may, one fact at least that doctors and moralists are likely to agree on is that prevention is better than cure. But how to prevent unwanted pregnancies in an atmosphere of ever-increasing sexual freedom and social permissiveness? One problem is that sex sells, and it sells not only itself but other things as well. Whole industries thrive on the simple fact that people are interested in sex and react favourably to products projecting a sexy image. One industry in particular which knows this only too well is the beauty business.

Part Five

MONEY THROUGH FEAR

CHAPTER TEN

Beauty

Few people, if given the chance, would choose not to be beautiful. The childhood vision of the beautiful princess living happily ever after with her handsome prince is not easily shattered. The fairy tale in which the hero falls for a girl with acne and split ends whose breath smells and who tips the scales at 200 pounds has yet to be written. In the world of dreams beauty is the key to success, happiness, marriage, even life itself, for to be beautiful is to be loved.

Beauty is an elusive and indefinable attribute. It lies not only in the eye of the beholder but in the eye of the beholden as well, for the image we have of ourselves is every bit as important as the image we present to others. If the blonde girl with false black eyelashes believes that they make her eyes look large and mysterious she will hold her head high and feel on top of the world, even if the people who pass her in the street are convinced that she is no more than a common tart. But the image we have of ourselves is also conditioned by others, so that if enough people tell her that they are terrible the girl will finally throw her eyelashes away. In the world of beauty nothing is certain, for what is beautiful today may be ugly tomorrow and yesterday's idol may be today's outcast. The best one can do is to strive for beauty within the accepted standards of one's group, whether this means wearing an Afro hairstyle and plum-coloured lipstick or the latest Sassoon cut and no lipstick at all.

Whatever the particular ideal one sets out to achieve, one will not get very far without the help of money. Beauties are rarely born but are often made, and the modern cosmetics industry thrives by convincing everyone that behind that plain exterior there lies a new, beautiful you just waiting to be discovered. For the price of a jar of cream, a bottle of pills, a new hair colour or a fresh lip gloss, strange and marvellous things will begin to happen. The man of your dreams will miraculously appear at your window on a white horse, a broken love affair will be magically healed, your husband will come back from the office and whisk you off to the sea for a midnight stroll followed by a night of passion. Who could resist such tempting promises? Anyone can spare a few pounds if it is the price of salvation.

In the United States, beauty is a seven-billion-dollar industry and growing fast, while Britons spend almost as much per capita on beauty products and services as the Americans do. The business of being beautiful has achieved singular importance, especially in capitals such as London and New York where how you look often matters just as much as, if not more than, who you are. Not surprisingly the highest income groups devote very much more time and money to this area of their lives than the low income groups do, and social surveys indicate that expenditure on beauty products rises significantly with an increase in income. There is no end to the possibilities of self-improvement, and for those with the time and money to spare, being beautiful can become a way of life in itself. A supreme example of such devotion is Luciana Avedon, the former Princess Pignatelli, who reveals in her *Beautiful People's Beauty Book*:

'What nature skipped, I supplied—so much so that sometimes I cannot remember what is real and what is fake. More important, neither can anyone else.'

Without the money to do it, however, this happy state of affairs could never have been reached, for the beautiful Luciana Avedon who sat down to write her book had, at 35, had her nose re-shaped, face and eyes lifted, breasts operated on, and had spent an incalculable fortune on massage, exercise, spas, health farms and expensive doctors—all these things she freely admits. Sadly, crows' feet, sagging chins, wrinkled skin and bags under the eyes are not dispelled by creams and lotions any more than dreams come true after using Badedas. The only effective weapon in the fight against ageing is money.

The amount of money that can, and indeed must, be spent by anyone seriously devoted to the pursuit of youth and beauty is quite beyond the imagination of the average wage-earner. A typical day in the life of a Beautiful Person starts with a visit to an exercise salon followed by a sauna and/or massage; after lunch a hairdo and facial are followed by a beauty bath and careful preparations for the evening's entertainment. Such a day would cost, in London, upwards of £15 and in New York considerably more. A twenty-minute consultation with Erno Laszlo, New York's most famous skin specialist, costs $75 and must be arranged six months in advance; a haircut at one of America's top hairdressing salons can leave you $50 lighter, while a hand-sewn wig made to order costs between $400 and $500. In spite of the price it is not unusual for women to have a wig wardrobe consisting of 30, 40, or even 50 different models. Where beauty is concerned every need can be supplied, every whim satisfied. There is even an Eyelash Studio in New York where, after a $10 consultation, clients can have individual lashes applied for a fee of between $25 and $50. The process is usually repeated twice a month.

Such things are taken for granted by serious followers of Narcissus and are no more exceptional than the never-ending stream of bank-notes that goes on creams and lotions, perfumes and powders. In the pursuit of beauty no area must be left unattended, every wrinkle must be routed, every surplus pound of flesh dispersed. It is a task that demands dedication as well as riches, and for those with idle days it serves to lend a sense of purpose to their lives.

Daily routines are of course only the beginning. The passing of time calls for more serious action as the last blush of youth begins to fade. The most powerful weapons in the beauty game are also the most expensive, but for those with the necessary capital there is a remedy for nearly everything. Faces can be lifted, breasts swelled or diminished and cheek hollows filled out; features can be restructured, ears pinned back, fat removed and blemishes banished; hair can be transplanted, bony hands corrected, bags under the eyes dispelled. The promises of cosmetics are nothing compared to the achievements of surgery, for no matter what offence nature has wrought someone somewhere is ready with a remedy, provided of course that you can afford the fee.

The most common operation in cosmetic surgery is the face-lift which, performed in London by a good plastic surgeon, costs around £250. In New York it is more likely to be somewhere between $1,000 and $5,000. The operation takes a month to six weeks to recover from, and to be really effective it must be repeated every few years. Women are not the only ones to have their faces lifted, for the growth of male fashion-consciousness has brought about a resurrection of masculine vanity. The current social climate links beauty with youth regardless of sex, and now that plastic surgery is no longer a forbidden subject more and more men are giving thought to improving their appearance in this way. Just as men who use after-shave and wear bright colours are no longer suspect, so there is nothing wrong with removing a flabby tummy or disguising baldness with the aid of a surgeon's knife. Nature alone cannot do these things for nature alone is content to let us grow old.

However miraculous the results of cosmetic surgery may be, there is certainly nothing enjoyable about it. The desire to be pampered remains unfulfilled in clinical surroundings, so that no matter how pleased the patient may be with his or her new self, the desire to withdraw to a beauty farm for a week to ten days to be fussed over may be hard to resist.

To most women and many men a beauty farm represents the ultimate in luxury. What could be more marvellous than to withdraw completely from the humdrum world of reponsibilities and pressures to a perfectly relaxed realm inhabited only by those who seek the glorification of the body beautiful? Once inside a health farm every adult becomes a precious, pampered child.

Such luxury is dearly bought. In the United States a week in a fashionable beauty farm costs about $800 without extras, and though this is very much more costly than in Britain, a week in a comparable British institution is still expensive by most people's standards. During the Christmas of 1970/71 I spent ten days in Buxted Park, a beautiful retreat in Sussex which has sadly now been sold. The bill came to £80 for an experience which was both funny and sad, uplifting and demoralizing.

I drove down from London on a cold and grey December afternoon. The letter of confirmation, enclosing a simple map, had urged that I be there between 3.00 p.m. and 6.00 p.m. The traffic out of London was bad and my sense of direction more than usually inept, and I turned up the radio in order to smother my mounting impatience. I was suddenly a schoolgirl again, facing my first day at a new school, and I was anxious not to offend my unknown superiors by arriving late.

I made it with ten minutes to spare. The large wooden sign saying simply Buxted Park stood at the end of a tree-lined drive and could be seen from a long way off. The trees had shed their leaves long ago and the naked branches looked depressing in the grey half-light, but I could see that in the summer they would form a beautiful green avenue.

The drive must have been about half a mile long, uphill all the way. The house lay hidden until the final curve had been topped, and then suddenly revealed itself, large, gracious, a nobleman's country seat. I could not help wondering, as I walked towards the elegant front door, how they could have allowed it to be painted purple.

I was greeted at the reception desk by a cheerful, bouncy girl who must have been at least a stone overweight. She asked me to sign the visitors' book and led me through a long, carpeted corridor and up a wide, sweeping staircase to my room. The name Johann Sebastian Bach was written in fancy gold lettering on the door. 'All the rooms are called after someone famous,' said the girl helpfully. Then, 'You'd better hurry up and change or you'll miss your consultation. The doctor goes home at six.' One more bright smile and she was gone.

The room was simple but cosy. A bright bedcover spread

its colour through the room and the large expanse of window was curtained in chintz. I noticed that there were three mirrors, one on the dressing table, a full-length one inside the wardrobe and a third one in the bathroom. I had no time for further contemplation because the telephone rang and a crisp female voice said, 'Your consultation is in five minutes. If you put on your robe, I'll send someone up to show you the way.'

I found the robe, blue towelling and quite enormous, hanging behind the bathroom door. As I was uncertain about what to take off I stripped down to my bra and pants and proceeded to swathe myself in the ridiculous mass of towelling. The girl who came to fetch me was sympathetic. 'We don't get many patients of your size,' she said looking me up and down. 'The robes are even too small for some of them.' I felt as if I had been awarded a good mark and let my thoughts dwell smugly on the elephantine creatures who had previously inhabited my robe as I followed her downstairs to the doctor's consulting room.

'You are four pounds overweight', he announced flatly, 'but the trouble is that you really need to lose it on your arms and upper legs.' I looked with distaste at the offending limbs which seemed suddenly to have swollen to grotesque proportions. 'I think diet and special exercise would be the best thing for you,' and he began to write busily on a large sheet of paper. He was, I considered, strangely unreal. Neither his voice nor his face revealed any emotion, his eyes were expressionless and the colour of his hair merged so completely with his skin that it was hard to tell where one ended and the other began. Like any true disciple, his calling had given him an unearthly quality. I tried to imagine him making love but the thought was almost blasphemous.

'I'm putting you on hot water and lemon for breakfast, half a grapefruit for lunch and soup in the evening,' he said sternly as though he had guessed my thoughts and was punishing me for my lack of reverence. 'Try to get lots of exercise. I'll see you again the day after tomorrow.' He handed me my miserable little diet sheet and I was dismissed.

The following morning I was woken at eight o'clock by a girl bearing a large breakfast tray. On closer inspection it turned out to contain nothing more than a saucer of lemon slices, a pot of hot water and a piece of paper informing me of the day that lay ahead—massage at nine o'clock, exercises at ten and a sauna in the afternoon. There was also an optional foot bath and something called music and colour in the evening. With a burst of enthusiasm I left the lemon untouched and wandered downstairs for my first appointment with beauty.

I had intended to ask the girl a whole string of questions but the massage was so superb that beneath her expert touch and the luxury of sweet-smelling oils I fell asleep. When I woke it was with a deep sense of peace and well-being and I began to understand why people were prepared to spend so much money to come here. My first day had hardly begun and already I felt more beautiful. 'Is it your first time here?' asked the baby-faced young girl. I nodded, then remembering who was supposed to be asking the questions I said to her with genuine curiosity, 'Don't you ever get sick of the sight of naked flesh?' She considered the question carefully. 'Sometimes,' she admitted, 'but it's worth it when you see results.'

The exercise class gave me my first glimpse of some of the other people in the group. It was a mixed class taken by a cheerful, red-faced man with a pot belly, but in spite of his hearty encouragement the atmosphere was still stiff with self-consciousness. Few people possessed of natural dignity are able to relish the prospect of lying with their backsides in the air in front of members of the opposite sex, however attractive their rear view may be. The ordeal lasted for half an hour, at the end of which time I had estimated that most of the people were between their late thirties and early fifties and that women outnumbered men by about three to one. Any closer inspection had to wait until twelve o'clock when those on a diet gathered to collect their meagre rations.

Hunger was beginning to gnaw at my empty stomach, and in spite of the fact that I viewed the prospect of half a grapefruit with distaste I was still the first to arrive. I could see from the trays of food laid out on the table that some people were even less fortunate than I, having only hot water and lemon, while a few lucky ones were granted the luxury of a fresh salad.

Most of the people who wandered in in twos and threes were well-dressed and well-spoken. They included business-men, housewives, actors and actresses, a fashion model, a film producer and a sixteen-year-old schoolgirl. Not all of them were obviously overweight but it was soon clear from the snatches of conversation that carried through the room that all of them were passionately concerned about every-thing to do with diet.

'I've lost four pounds in two days,' said the middle-aged actress proudly, sleeking down her strawberry blonde hair with a well-manicured hand. Her companion looked up from her glass of carrot juice. 'I've lost six,' she replied shortly, and they both fell silent.

'The marvellous thing is', boomed the company director

from the other end of the room, 'that my rheumatism has quite disappeared. I feel like a new man.' His partner nodded miserably, 'I feel like a plate of steak and chips,' he said sadly.

'You know I've lost two whole inches off my hips', gushed the model delightedly to no-one in particular, 'and I just know that by the time I leave here my thighs will be absolutely perfect.' She stretched out her legs and sighed contentedly as she toyed with a spoonful of cottage cheese. 'It's so super—my agent will be thrilled to bits!'

And so it went on. No reference was made to work, families, or professional interests. No word was exchanged on books, plays, films or indeed any subject outside the individuals' immediate surroundings. Talk was only about how one feels, how much weight one has lost or wants to lose, how this diet compares with that one. Whatever differences people may have had in their private lives, once inside that purple front door nothing existed but their own bodies.

I was wondering why such a hive of self-indulgence should produce so many miserable faces (I had heard no-one laugh since my arrival the previous day) when a foreign voice close to my ear said, 'Would you like a game of table tennis?' I looked up to see a tall, olive-skinned gentleman smiling at me. 'All right,' I said, remembering what the doctor had said about exercise. Action would probably help me to forget about food as well, I thought, as I followed him downstairs to the gym.

His name was Reza and he was Persian. 'I come here every year for eight years', he explained as he shot the ball to the other end of the room, 'and I always lose fourteen pounds. I then put it back on at the rate of about a pound a month so that by the time I come back here I have the same fourteen pounds to get off.'

'Can't you ever keep your weight down when you leave here?' I asked sympathetically.

'But I never try,' he replied happily, obviously surprised at the question. 'Why should I make myself miserable all the year round when I can come here and pay someone to do it for me in eight days? It's so much simpler.'

'But what would you do if you were poor?' I insisted, hoping to make him feel ashamed of his laziness. He smiled at me. 'If I were poor,' he explained patiently, 'then I would not be fat.'

Downstairs in the sauna I again experienced the same sensation of well-being that I had felt that morning. This time I began to realize that it was the sheer luxury of having time stand still, the complete dedication of the silent white-gowned women who pampered and soothed, that made this haven of beauty a place that people with enough money came back to again and again. The absence of pressure was in itself beyond price for many of them, for it created an atmosphere in which they could do nothing but abandon themselves to the pursuit of their own well-being. Like sex, complete surrender was the key to success.

This feeling was reinforced by the four o'clock foot bath which was communal and unintentionally very comic. The sight of a dozen assorted men and women solemnly treading water with their robes clutched tightly above their knees was like something out of an old-fashioned comedy film. 'This is marvellous for the circulation,' encouraged the instructor. 'Get your knees up as high as you can—one two, one two, that's the way.'

'Will this really make us more beautiful?' I ventured to ask the woman marching next to me. 'Of course,' she replied, 'as long as you believe in it.' Her remark lingered in my mind and I began to realize that if you pay enough, then you believe in anything.

That evening we all gathered in the luxurious little cinema to find out what was meant by music and colour. First of all there was a lecture by the same man who had been in charge of the foot-bath. 'You are not here only to relax and improve your bodies,' he told us. 'In order to achieve complete well-being you must also relax your minds.' We were urged to forget any problems we might have, personal or professional, and simply let our thoughts drift like leaves in a summer breeze. Then came the music, classical and restful, and at the same time a large television screen was filled with an ever-shifting kaleidoscope of graceful, soothing colours. Who could possibly worry about a drop in share prices or an incompetent au pair in the face of such expert and subtle seduction? By the time the last note had faded more than half the listeners were sound asleep.

And so the days passed, one much the same as the next. When I had lost seven pounds I was allowed to graduate to the dining room, but the people there were thin and miserable, and I preferred life with the dieters who had now grown a little more cheerful. Some would steal off to the village for a forbidden cup of coffee or pint of beer and recount their adventures with all the bravado of unrepentant sinners. At that time we were so conditioned to the idea of lemon and beetroot juice that things like alcohol, bread and chocolate seemed infinitely worse than the worst kind of sexual perversion. In this realm of beauty worshippers, anything that prevented the achievement of physical perfection was automatically regarded as the ultimate sin.

I was sent back to the world ten days after my arrival,

nine pounds lighter in weight and £80 lighter in pocket. I felt strangely purified, as though I had re-entered the womb to be born all over again, but I also sensed that, were I ever to return, the lack of novelty would lead to excruciating boredom. Those who go regularly to beauty farms have different values from mine. They are true believers who believe not only in the beauty industry but in the importance of being as beautiful as possible. Beauty may be only skin deep but to them it is the surface that matters. Why do they do it? What is the whole complex beauty industry really for? Kathrin Perutz answers that question in her excellent book *Beyond the Looking Glass*:

'To be beautiful—for what? To be fucked. Why? To look more beautiful. Why? That way lies money.'

So it comes back again to money. We need money to look beautiful, and we need to look beautiful to attract money. What a crazy vicious circle it is.

CHAPTER ELEVEN

Art

Art is a form of human communication and one of the purest expressions of the spirit of man. But art is also a form of international currency whose value is not eroded by time, and this simple fact has been enough to turn the art world into a market place and beautiful things into objects of investment. The sad part is that, to a public punch-drunk with inflation, the investment aspect tends to be more important than the object.

This attitude is sustained by a number of factors such as the widespread publicity given to rising saleroom prices and the impression created by the mass media that what matters most about a work of art is its value. Headlines such as 'Record price paid for Henry Moore', '£1 million paintings recovered by Italian police', and feature articles like 'The never-ending search for a bonanza in the boxroom' positively encourage people to think of art in terms of bank notes.

The effect of this money-polluted atmosphere is well illustrated by the story of a rich New York socialite who, in the spring of 1972, began legal proceedings against the Parke Bernet Galleries in downtown Manhattan. Her complaint was that she had unwittingly sold, through them, a Raphael masterpiece for $325 in the belief that it was practically worthless. The lady in question set about demanding $12 million as the painting's true value, $36 million in damages as a result of alleged conspiracy, $3 million for expenses sustained in establishing the painting's authenticity, and a touching $1 million for 'emotional stress and discomfort'. She quite forgot to mention whether or not she liked the painting.

The U.S. dollar has in fact been a fundamental driving force behind rising art prices, particularly as far as Old Masters are concerned. In order to make up for the lack of artistic tradition of which they were so conscious, the Americans set out to import a cultural heritage from Europe. Since the New World's lack of tradition was not matched by a corresponding lack of dollars, a steady flow of masterpieces soon began across the Atlantic. At the same time prices in Europe began to rise, not only because the Americans had more money and were prepared to spend it but also because they had no artistic standards by which to measure prices. The only standard they had was the dollar, and a work of art was therefore worth as many dollars as were necessary to buy it. As paintings were sold and resold, prices were pushed higher and higher and aesthetic values became more and more difficult to reconcile with the spiralling figures. It seemed that Oscar Wilde's gentleman was not alone in knowing 'the price of everything and the value of nothing'.

One must not forget, however, that the power of the dollar was strongly reinforced by the different attitudes of the British and American governments. In Britain works of art were until very recently treated as part of an individual's wealth for tax purposes, and in spite of repeated appeals by artistic institutions, no concessions were granted on estate duty for generosity in donating a painting to a museum or gallery. There was therefore no incentive for an individual to enrich the nation's store of art treasures in this way, in fact it was positively in his interest to sell whatever he had acquired for ready cash and spend the money. In the United States, however, very favourable concessions have always been granted to those who present works of art to public collections, so that the combined effect of this legislation was to speed the movement of art across the Atlantic in search of the highest prices and then to keep it there.

Safeguards do exist to prevent British art treasures of particular worth from leaving the country, but even they depend on money and the last word inevitably rests with the party able to write out the fattest cheque. The fact that an export licence can be refused by the authorities if a matching British offer is made within a specified period is of little value when the specified period is three months and the market price runs into millions. The £2,310,000 paid at Christie's for a Velasquez portrait in November 1970 was more than the entire year's purchase grant of £2 million allowed by the Treasury for all the museums and galleries in Britain put together. Viewed in this light it is easy to see how the power of money can dominate the art market.

The implications of this state of affairs are perhaps not immediately apparent, for they go far beyond the obvious fact that art finds its way to the highest bidder. If one looks again at the Velasquez portrait sold to an American for £2,310,000 one begins to see something of the effect that money can have on an artist's work. The painting, a portrait of Velasquez's mulatto assistant Juan de Pareja, was painted as an honest, serious record of a friend. It was completed at the time when Velasquez received the commission to paint Pope Innocent X in 1649, and the feelings of love and friendship that inspired it found expression in the beauty of the finished work. The fact that it was also a masterpiece was incidental, and any thought of money, needless to say, totally absent.

The painting was still a beautiful work of art when it was sold at Christie's in 1801 for 39 guineas, but when the hammer fell at the same saleroom one hundred and sixty-nine years later for more than £2,300,000 the portrait was no longer the same. Its real value had been marred and never again could it be looked upon and admired as a beautiful work of art. From the moment the hammer fell and it acquired the title of the most expensive painting in the world, Velasquez's portrait of his mulatto assistant became a curiosity, a thing to be stared at, quoted in the book of records and cited in the price indices. Even if other paintings eventually outprice it the damage can never be undone. The painting will for ever bear its price tag like a scar.

It would be wrong to create the impression that money is always a destructive force in the art world, for this is not so. The case of Mrs Rosemary Cattrell proves conclusively that money can also be constructive if approached in the right way. Mrs Cattrell inherited a painting from her uncle when he died in 1954 and though neither she nor her husband liked it they felt obliged to hang it on their living room wall. It stayed there for fifteen years until Mrs Cattrell, an art teacher, decided that her uncle's memory had been sufficiently honoured for her to be able to sell it and buy something that she really liked. The Cattrells therefore took the painting to Sothebys where it was discovered to be the work of Hans Baldung, a sixteenth-century German master, and where it was subsequently sold for a staggering £224,000. Needless to say the Cattrells were delighted, not because they had unknowingly been harbouring a masterpiece for fifteen years but because something they had genuinely disliked had unexpectedly provided the means for them to buy, as Mr Cattrell said afterwards, 'some pictures that we actually like—more modern works'. He added, 'The most attractive paintings I have are those by my daughter, aged seven.'

Few people are as unaffected by the price tag of a painting as the Cattrells, however, particularly when it comes to more modern works where judgment is even more influenced by the amount of money involved. A painting or sculpture by an unknown artist commands more respect when it is highly priced than when it is cheap, simply because the untrained eye looks to the money value as an indication of artistic worth. The whole purpose of the work is thus totally destroyed as it is reduced to the level of a commercial proposition, a unit of buying and selling which is tossed from hand to hand in accordance with prevailing market trends. It is hardly surprising that many present-day artists, the younger ones in particular, are increasingly concerned about the way in which creative experiences are systematically transformed into gold.

One person who feels especially strongly about this is André Durand, a young Canadian painter who has been living and working in London for the past five years. A slight figure with a sensitive face and unkept curly hair, André lives with two cats and a dog in a practically empty Victorian flat with vast rooms and high ceilings. Every available area of wall space is covered with his own large canvases, and apart from a sofa, a couple of chairs and a bed, the only piece of furniture in the flat is an enormous easel. André's work is surprisingly classical, usually depicting the human form, and he does an increasing amount of portrait work as well. Perhaps it is the intensely personal nature of his art that makes him so concerned about the impersonal way in which it reaches the public. In his view, as he explains, the root cause of the increasing commercialization of art lies in the system of marketing it.

'If you follow the process in stages you will see what I mean. The artist first of all creates a painting or series of paintings which he wants to show to the public. But in order to show them he needs a gallery sufficiently interested in his work to promote it. That in itself is bad enough—why should his future depend on the judgment of one or two men?—but the crux of the matter is that galleries are commercial enterprises and their primary concern is money. Therefore, even more important than interest is the fact that the work should be considered saleable. Art is immediately reduced to the level of a market commodity. In fact commercial considerations can even overrule personal taste, and a gallery may well reject work that it considers worthwhile on the grounds of limited appeal. It applies the other way round too, and galleries are equally prepared to accept mediocre work if they think it will sell.

'The dependence of the artist on a gallery to promote his work is therefore the first weak link in the chain. The second is the critic, whose words not only influence what people see but the way in which they see it. A critic can surround two black lines on a white canvas with such a glowing aura of respect that people feel stupid if they do not admire it too, and positively fall over themselves to pay the exorbitant prices demanded. It is like the Emperor's new clothes—no-one has the courage to stand up and proclaim that it is just a confidence trick. Equally a critic can destroy an artist's work by publicly denouncing it as rubbish. It may well be that he is simply unable to appreciate it, but his verdict means that many other people will be prevented from appreciating it too because his judgment will go with them to the exhibition.

'The worst aspect of the current system is that there is no contact between the artist and his public any more. If we could only do away with indirect selling, art would come back into its own once again and cease to be a commercial operation. I would like to see the profit-orientated middlemen disappear altogether so that people can be free to go straight to an artist and choose a painting or work out an idea for something they feel they would like to own. After all a painting is an expression of the owner as much as of the artist and if both are involved from the start it stands to reason that the result will be much more meaningful for both of them.

'Personally I try to involve money as little as possible in my work. I would much rather barter than sell because a painting without a price tag is really a painting and nothing else, but when I do sell my work money is always a secondary consideration. What matters most is whether the person really responds to the painting and genuinely wants to own it. If the response is right, the price is something that can be decided between us, and should he really be unable to afford it then I am often happy to let him have it for nothing. But if the response is not right and I feel that he wants the painting just as a status symbol or as an investment then I have no qualms about charging him according to his motives. People who have no love of art deserve to be exploited, because they themselves are exploiting the artists in the first place.

'There is no doubt that money does influence people's judgment, in fact some people don't even look at a painting properly until they know how much it costs. The price is a stepping-stone on an uncertain path; it provides a standard by which to assess good and bad, like and dislike.

But they miss the whole point of the painting which is to promote spontaneous reaction.

'The trouble is that people are afraid to be spontaneous in case they make fools of themselves. They have been so conditioned, by galleries and the press, to accept the judgment of others that when they have nothing, not even a price to guide them, they are lost.'

Not everyone feels as André Durand does. One person who strongly disagrees is David Wynne, one of Britain's most successful sculptors, whose work includes the now famous 'Four Men' which has become the trademark of the Taylor Woodrow company, and the head of Prince Charles commissioned for his investiture as Prince of Wales in 1969. Now in his forties, David lives with his family in an informal sprawling house on the outskirts of London. In spite of his success there is little sign of affluence and the sculptor himself is happiest in jeans and a tee-shirt both in and out of his studio. His work has been exhibited all over the world, but in spite of the high prices he is now able to command, David Wynne is adamant in his belief that money and art are completely separate.

'Money has no power to affect art in any way because it has nothing at all to do with it. Art is on a completely different level from all the things that are commonly referred to as the art world. Galleries, salerooms, art dealers, art schools, art historians, none of them have anything to do with art and nothing that they do can possibly touch it. If all the galleries and art schools closed tomorrow and every art critic blew his brains out, it would make no difference to art at all.

'I don't resent galleries in the least; they work hard for their 40% or whatever they charge and they are more than welcome to it. It certainly isn't true that they affect what people buy any more than the critics do—they simply make it possible for a great many people to see things that they could never afford to buy. I have never had a favourable write-up in the whole of my career and yet my work has sold steadily and increasingly over the years. People don't need critics to tell them what to buy.

'I don't care if people buy my work for investment reasons or any other reason; the art is unaffected by motives just as it is unaffected by money. In the same way I don't believe it is possible for a great work of art to be debased by its price. A Raphael, Titian or Henry Moore is still the same work of art whatever it is sold for. If the publicity given to a particularly high price makes people look at the work for the wrong reasons then the chances are that they wouldn't have looked at it at all otherwise. It is surely better for them to see it with their minds cluttered up with figures than not to see it at all.

'The work of a true artist is completely unaffected by financial considerations. An artist creates because he has something to say, and he continues to create regardless of whether his work sells or not. Look at Van Gogh—even if he had been paid £2 million for a painting in his lifetime he would still have produced the work he did and he would still have cut his ear off. Money is irrelevant.

'Of course there are always people with little or no talent waiting to jump on a promising bandwagon, and many insignificant painters and sculptors succeed in getting good reviews and selling their work for high prices. It's the same with pop music, the number of really talented musicians is incredibly small compared with the number who are making money out of it. But that again has nothing to do with art, that is just commerce.

'I agree that it can be easy to confuse the two. For

instance, if my main aim was to make money I would do very much more work than I do now. I would probably do twenty heads a year instead of six, and no-one I'm sure would notice the slightest difference in creative achievement except me.

'The reason why people in the West get taken in so easily and so often is that they don't know how to look at art in the first place. Their minds are too preoccupied with problems of verbal communication and wondering what to say. That doesn't happen in the East—an Oriental knows how to respond to art without feeling the need to say anything about it. They don't have this wave of new intellectuals casting about in their minds for significant comments to make.

'But in spite of the fact that work that sells is not necessarily art and vice versa, I firmly believe that there is always room for the best in every society. It may not sell in the artist's lifetime, but that does not make it any the less of an achievement. It is not selling art that matters, it is creating it that is important. The world's masterpieces are not for sale anyway—you can't buy the Acropolis, the Duomo in Florence, Beethoven's Seventh Symphony. Art is there, it exists; money doesn't.'

David Wynne is right, of course; money does not exist. But that does not stop the gallery handling his work from making sure that his prices never go down. In the same way it does not stop people from stealing beautiful paintings and cutting them up to sell for profit, nor does it prevent them from buying a Henry Moore and locking it up in the safe as an investment. Art may have nothing to do with money as far as the artist is concerned, but what happens to the art when it leaves the studio indicates that a great many people think otherwise.

Happily, however, there are still those who do not take part in the money game at all. They are the people with ideals, with special callings, who neither crave money nor use it in any other way than to survive. In the last part of this book some of these people talk about life without money, and why they prefer it.

Part Six

PEACE WITHOUT MONEY

CHAPTER TWELVE

The commune

Communes are hazy places that hover uncertainly on the fringes of society. Those within society who bother to think about them at all usually dismiss them as dens of iniquity inhabited by idle, long-haired flower children who all sleep together and never wash. These undesirables either live off the state at the taxpayers' expense or else they deal in drugs and grow fat on the ill-gotten gains.

All these things may well be true, but they are not, as this kind of prejudiced thinking implies, necessarily true. There is in fact no such thing as a typical commune, and if the members of the commune movement have anything in common at all, it is simply the desire to live together in groups. Group life can mean the sharing of a house by individuals or families, with everyone taking an equal part in the domestic chores, or it can centre round a particular philosophy or religion, a political ideal, a specialist craft or trade. In all the groups there is a desire to be dissociated from the competitive order of things, and to replace material values with those of a more lasting kind—religious, idealistic or artistic.

That does not mean to say that money is discarded: in many working communes it is not unusual for individual earnings to be kept and spent in the normal way. Some communes, however, have been broken up by the dissatisfaction caused by wide divergences in people's earnings, and the most usual arrangement, therefore, is to pool everyone's income and, after deducting expenses such as food and housekeeping, to divide the money equally between all members of the group.

Many communes are self-supporting, and have little need for money; others, anxious to realize more far-reaching ideals, find that they cannot do without it. Such a commune is the one in which Frances lives and which she founded in a respectable Oxfordshire neighbourhood just over two years ago.

Frances is 47 and an anarchist. She lives with six similarly minded adults, two children and three cats in a rambling white farmhouse a few miles from Oxford. Six of the seven adults are couples, though not married, and there is one extra man who has come here with his baby son. The other child, a five-year-old girl, belongs to Frances' 24-year-old daughter Sheila, who also lives here as part of the group. Other people come and go from time to time, either singly or in pairs, but these seven adults and two children consider themselves a constant unit.

The whitewashed farmhouse in which they all live dates back to the fifteenth century in parts, but it is sadly neglected with faded oak beams and a crumbling thatched roof. The paintwork, too, is weatherworn and peeling and the overgrown front lawn is littered with tools and broken toys so that anyone crossing it must pick his way with care. A battered blue minivan parked on the unmade drive has a sign in the back window saying 'Support your local planet'.

Inside, the house is larger than it looks, with long winding corridors and three flights of stairs making it seem larger still. Bedrooms seem to go on for ever as hallways turn abruptly instead of coming to an expected end, and the general lack of furniture and ornaments intensifies the feeling of space still further. As a house it is marvellous, with rough plastered walls, uneven floors and crooked beamed ceilings, but sadly, disappointingly, it has now been turned into nothing less than a human pigsty.

The most appalling place is the kitchen. A large, high-ceilinged room with a bare wooden floor and damp on the walls, it presents a picture of unmitigated filth and decay. The gas stove is covered in grime, and the sink, chipped and peeling, is full of dirty pots and pans. A long wooden table is strewn with bits and pieces of leftover food, scraps of butter on dirty plates, open jars of pickle and jam, half-eaten slices of bread. On the floor, which looks as though it has never been swept, two cats are busily drinking milk out of a soup plate. ('We don't see anything wrong with animals using the same plates as humans,' Frances remarks later.) Rotting food lies on some open shelves in a corner by the window and the smell of decay mingles with the smell of dirt. There are flies everywhere.

The rest of the house is in a similar state of neglect and disarray. Worn patches of odd carpet thrown down here and there, the floors littered with rubbish, books, dolls, empty boxes, tattered pieces of clothing. Not only is there a shortage of furniture, but what there is is thread-bare in the extreme with stuffing coming out of the arm-chairs and holes in the worn-out sofas. Upstairs the beds are unmade, exposing greying, crumpled sheets and pillow-cases, and where there are curtains these too are dirty and ill-fitting. There are no mirrors and no cosmetics of any kind anywhere in the house, and the only picture on any of the walls is a large, blown-up photograph of a young girl walking naked through a field of knee-high grass. It is as though anything which interferes with the natural course of things is necessarily an evil.

A young girl of about 16 emerges briefly from the downstairs living room. She passes without a smile, inviting no pleasantries, but she looks gentle all the same with pale, fragile features and long, wispy hair. Her sleeveless cotton dress is matted with dirt and on her feet she wears a pair of old canvas shoes, torn and full of holes. She goes through into the kitchen, her fleeting appearance having made the lack of personal objects in the house even more striking. There are no books or photographs, no records or paintings, no mementoes or sentimental objects of any kind. There is not even a bowl of fruit or a vase of flowers, though the tangled grounds at the back look well able to provide both. Clearly these people have no time for material things, but even if their life-style is based on sincere political thinking the squalor that surrounds them is likely to deter many people from seeking to discover just what it is they are trying to achieve.

Frances appears in the doorway and beckons me into the smaller of the two living rooms. It ought to be cosy but furnished as it is with a rotting table, two threadbare armchairs with ragged covers hanging off them and a filthy sofa charred by cigarette burns, the result is not really inviting. As she talks Frances frequently scratches herself vigorously, usually on her scalp but often rolling up her trousers to get to her bare legs. The automatic way in which she sets about it indicates that it is something she is well used to doing.

Physically she is not an attractive woman. The contours of her face are hard and well-defined, the chin pointed, the nose abruptly turned up at the end. The hollows under her cheekbones are exaggerated by a sallow skin and greying black hair cut in a severe pudding-basin hair cut. Her dark eyes, lined beyond her years and faintly bloodshot, reveal no tenderness even when she speaks of those she has loved. Her skin has clearly never been touched by make-up and there is no attempt at beautification or adornment. Her hands, thick, working-man's hands with stubby, dirt-lined fingernails, are never still for more than a few seconds, and as she talks (with a surprisingly old-fashioned upper class accent) her wiry body is continually changing position.

'We bought this house', she begins abruptly, 'for £17,000 in cash. The money was raised by pooling all our savings, and borrowing from our friends, in fact one girl (she pronounces it gel) actually gave us £3,000 because there was nothing else she wanted to do with it. All we have to pay back now is £3,000 from someone else.

'Personally I'm not really sure about having a house, having spent most of my life living in a caravan. You are so much closer to nature living on the land, and there are no material hassles like rent, rates and bills to worry about. But we decided that we needed a permanent home, a base if you like, to operate from and when we saw this place it seemed just perfect.

'I don't think that buying a house is giving in to the capitalist system, not since we were careful to form a limited company to buy it so that it belongs to all of us. Since most of us have jobs—two of the girls work in a macrobiotic restaurant and one of the boys works on the land—we all contribute an equal amount of £6.25 a week, or £5 if we share a room, to pay off the loan and run the house. It works very well.

'You must understand that everyone in this commune believes passionately in equality, that is the centre of our philosophy and the starting point for all our actions. By equality we mean equal pay and equal distribution of profits by companies which are controlled by the workers.

What we have at the moment is nothing more than a system based on exploitation and robbery. Wherever you look you see people working for a pittance in order to provide fat incomes for the men at the top. How many managers would be able to afford big houses, chauffeur-driven cars and first-class holidays abroad if it weren't for the workers who make the profits possible in the first place? But it's not only management which is exploiting the workers, everyone else is doing it too. Why, for example, should a television producer get paid ten times as much as a dustbinman? We can all live without television—in fact life would be a damn sight better without it—but we wouldn't be able to last long without someone to clear our houses and streets of rubbish. The television people, film producers, journalists, politicians, civil servants, all the professionals, are falsely rewarded for what they do and the result is that the workers, those who provide the essentials of life, are being robbed.

'Of course it takes someone like me who knows what poverty is to feel the injustice of it. I was never desperately poor, in fact I grew up in what you might call a typical middle-class suburban setting with a mathematician father, housewife mother and elder brother. But money was always important. I remember there were constant rows about it, and I think it was then that I began to sense something of the injustice caused by money. At that stage, of course, I was far too young to be able to evaluate it, let alone know what I wanted to do about it, but I did feel it, being poor, and I did think about it. Naturally those who are in control of the system or who benefit from it are not going to want to see it changed. But it's still wrong all the same. Every Rolls Royce is a symbol of injustice because no-one can buy a car like that without robbing others.

'I'm not denying that money is important—we couldn't have bought this house without it and I've nothing at all against money as a means of exchange—what's wrong is the way in which it is organized. Why should children or grandchildren for instance be able to benefit from something that their family did way back in the past? Apart from the fact that it's not good for them anyway it stops money from circulating by keeping it within the family group. The whole of the Western financial system is nothing but a farce.

'Here in this commune we are trying to do something to change all that, first of all by living as equals and secondly by divesting money of its power. On a day to day basis we do this by communal ownership of the house and everything in it, by contributing equal sums of money to meet our commitments each week and by doing away with the notion of leadership. No-one tells anyone else what to do here, whether it's cleaning the house or doing the shopping, and decisions are made by all of us after open discussion. If no-one feels like cleaning the house, well then it doesn't get done, that's all. But really it is my daughter's partner John who has given us the most exciting opportunity of putting our ideas into practice, because John comes from a wealthy family and without his money we wouldn't have been able to go much further than day to day living.

'I must just say that I don't know whether or not it was wrong of Sheila to get involved with him, feeling as she does about the rich; perhaps it was wrong. But the past is the past and cannot be undone in any case, so our task now is to move forward and find the best way of putting his money to good use. John himself is extremely concerned about the problem of power and money (although of course he didn't realize that it was a problem before he met me) and he really feels now that he has a responsibility towards the rest of society to use his money for the creation of a better system. In fact it is mostly thanks to him that we were able to buy this house in the first place.

'What we are hoping to do now is buy a local company (we have our eyes on one at the moment) and run it on the lines of co-ownership and profit-sharing by the workers. It would work just like this commune, without a leader and with everyone having an equal voice in the management and administration. People would put so much more into it if they knew that they were going to benefit directly from their efforts.'

For the first time Frances' eyes were bright with the excitement of her vision. I wondered how she would prevent these newly rich workers from rushing out and squandering their money on material status symbols, thus perpetuating the very system she was trying to destroy.

'Ah yes,' she replied, 'well, we have thought of that and I agree it could be a problem. We would just have to make sure that we only took on people with the same beliefs as ourselves. Ideally you see we would want to use the profits to start up other companies on the same lines. This means that the amount going to the workers would only be sufficient to allow them to live adequately until such time as everyone else had reached the same level. Anyone seeking to surround themselves with luxury at the expense of everyone else would simply not be welcome. It might be rather difficult at first, I admit, because most people probably are materialistic in their attitude, but that doesn't mean to say that acquisitiveness is a natural human attribute. It simply means that people have to be re-educated to think differently.

'There is altogether too much acceptance of things in the West. Take the tax system for example. I have no objection to paying taxes for education, hospitals, welfare and so on, but I do object most strongly to contributing to nonsense such as the space project and Concorde. There ought to be flag days for things like that so that people who are in favour of them can foot the bill. It's a flagrant abuse of people's freedom to use their money to further projects they don't approve of. If that's progress then we can well do without it.

'I must say I find most people's lives sadly lacking in purpose. They seem to move from this new gadget to that new machine without ever asking themselves what they are doing with their lives or indeed what life is all about. I have no patience with idleness of any kind, whether it's the idleness of the rich, the bored, the dropouts or the flower children. We are here for much too short a time to be able to waste a minute. Even my brother, who is younger than me, is beginning to feel this now. He comes here quite often and I'm sure he envies the fact that we are trying to do something positive to change things. Working in an office to provide enough money to bring up a family is really not enough.

'I never feel that I'm missing anything by not having nice clothes, new furniture and a shiny car. I ride around on a motor bike which I adore and which is ecologically far safer than a car anyway. All the same I always make sure that I have some savings tucked away somewhere so that I know I could buy something if I wanted to. It does happen sometimes that I feel like that, but usually just going into town to have a look at the shops is enough to satisfy me. The knowledge that I could buy whatever-it-is if I wanted to quite takes away the desire for it. I must admit that I rather enjoyed the one holiday I ever had abroad. It was with my present partner Simon, who is a 28-year-old graduate and has been living with me for nearly ten years, but I doubt if we will do it again. We can't afford it.

'Anyway things like holidays, status, even clothing, washing and cooking, all the things that make up the most part of other people's lives, are unimportant to us you see. It depends what your values are, and we in this commune have a purpose which completely outweighs everything else. If we can achieve even a small fraction of what we are trying to do then we will at least have done something in our lifetime to make the world a better place in which to live. And that's more than most people can say.'

It probably is more than most people can say, though everyone has his own concept of a better world. One person, however, who is doing good by any standard is Father Michaels, a gentle man of simple farming stock who has been a Roman Catholic priest for more than thirty years. During that time he has travelled the world, teaching, lecturing and listening to others. He has written several books, been actively involved in radio and television, and is well-known in religious circles for his independent outlook and progressive thinking. In fact, for someone in his position, his views are even more radical than Frances'.

CHAPTER THIRTEEN

The priesthood

The number of people entering religious orders today is far smaller than it was a generation or two ago. Opinions differ as to why this should be, but one view that is widely held and frequently expressed suggests that a major cause is the growing emphasis on material things. As money becomes more important, fewer people are inclined to enter a life where financial rewards are modest and luxury has no place. The Catholic church in particular is deeply concerned about the growth of money-consciousness and its adverse effect on admissions into the priesthood, understandably so when the Church already has its own internal crises to contend with and the present religious unrest is causing a growing number of priests to leave the Church anyway. That the ranks of the clergy should be diminished still further by outside forces is a cause of grave concern.

It is also faintly ironical because in practical terms the priesthood is far more attractive now than it was thirty years ago when Father Michaels entered the church. At that time the conditions he had to contend with during his seven years of study would have taxed the endurance of a saint. There is certainly no doubt in Father Michaels' mind that no-one today would be prepared to put up with the kind of life that he and his fellow initiates led at that time.

'Our freedom was severely restricted, visits to the cinema

were forbidden, exercise was limited to a bare minimum, and the food and conditions were frankly appalling,' he says. 'We once compared notes with some local borstal boys we used to visit, and they decided they were far better off in borstal than we were in our seminary. You really had to want the priesthood very badly to go through with it.'

Father Michaels did want the priesthood very badly. The eldest son of devout Catholic parents and the third of their six children, he decided at the age of eleven that he wanted to enter the church. He is now nearing fifty, a big, gentle man with humorous eyes and rugged good looks, and his life-style is probably more unconventional than that of most priests. Not only does he travel a great deal but he has also written several books and is very involved in radio and television programmes. Progressive in his outlook, he spends much of his time setting hymns and prayers to modern music, and in fact the most prominent feature of his book-lined living room is not the wooden crucifix hanging over the fireplace but the fine Spanish guitar standing next to it. This is Father Michaels' only luxury, this and his books, for though obviously not poor he chooses to live a very simple life. Money and the priesthood, he feels, do not go together.

'If I were Pope the first thing I would do is to hand over the Vatican and all the treasures of St Peter's to the Italian state and move out and go and live in a flat. Such riches should be put to a better purpose, particularly when so much of the world is starving, and in any case I have serious doubts about the Church, which is closest to Christ, being surrounded by such sumptuousness. I believe that the Pope himself leads a very simple life but even so I still feel that a world leader of the Church should not reside in a palace. I'm not saying he should live in a room somewhere in the slums—obviously he has diplomats and dignitaries to receive and he must see them in suitable surroundings—but he could live in a simple building and have access to a hall or reception room when necessary.

'I always feel it is wrong when I hear of members of the clergy dying and leaving maybe £20,000 or £30,000. In a rich parish, particularly in London, it is quite possible to save that kind of money, but it should be given away, put to some purpose, not stashed away in a bank somewhere. I think that is a terrible waste. If I ever wrote a best-seller and found myself with a sum of money like that, I would keep maybe £1,000 of it to live comfortably and give the rest to Oxfam or something. I think that, as followers of Christ, the clergy should try as far as possible to live the way that Christ lived and I'm sure that He would give away such money immediately, though of course He wouldn't even keep £1,000 for Himself.

'I think I feel rather guilty about money. It worries me that I have never known real poverty, never known what it is like to be destitute. I think that not having experienced this cuts me off from a large section of the population and makes it more difficult for me to communicate with those who are poor and starving and who come to me for help. I don't think it's as necessary for me to be rich because I feel at ease with the rich anyway and they with me. I think this is because, even though I have no riches in the material sense, I have riches of another kind and they feel this and respect it. In any case material possessions are so temporary—they are only lent to us for a short time. I care for the rich and am as concerned for them as I am for the poor; it's the person that matters, not what they have or who they are.

'I don't think that affluence is either a good thing or a bad thing in itself, any more than poverty is. It can be bad if it inspires greed and we become grasping and selfish, but it can also be good if it leads to helping others who are less fortunate than ourselves. In the same way poverty can be a bad thing if it causes bitterness but if it teaches us to appreciate the real values of life then it can be a very good thing indeed.

'From my own experience I would certainly say that money affects people's attitude towards religion. As they become more affluent, and therefore more sophisticated, better clothed and better fed, their attachment to the Church dwindles. If they go to church at all it is for social reasons, because in their community or society it is the thing to do, but really they find that the religious life has little to offer them any more. In countries where poverty is widespread, on the other hand, the number of people who turn to God, both as laymen and as priests, is far higher. I think this is a very great shame, but I also think it is partly the fault of the Church itself. People have been presented, and indeed are still being presented, with a medieval picture of God, God as an idol who must not be displeased, rather than a real force in their lives. It is not surprising therefore that most of them never get beyond what I call the lollipop stage of religion, looking upon God as a comforter and supporter in hard times. It is only to be expected that as they grow more sophisticated and better able to look after themselves they find that they can do without this kind of prop and they automatically assume that they have rejected religion. In fact they have really reached the stage where they can begin to understand God in a more mature and meaningful way. After all, as I said before, riches are only gifts, temporary gifts, and while they may well replace this rather childish picture of religion they cannot in any sense be a substitute for God.

'Perhaps I have been lucky in the way I was brought up. I was always taught to appreciate very simple pleasures, and I can honestly say that I have everything I could possibly want in life. Many people are not so lucky, and find themselves caught up in an existence which makes them both unhappy and confused. Often it does seem as though money is largely to blame, not because people have either too much or too little but simply because it becomes bigger than they are and they lose sight of what life is really about.

'One can see how this has led to the formation of the new Jesus movement which is now so strong among the young. Put in very general terms, what happened is this. A generation of God-fearing people grew up in times of war and hardship and slowly, through their own efforts and hard work, they managed to gather round them the material benefits of success—cars, nice houses, good clothes and so on. They then lavished these things on their children, anxious to spare them the hardship and suffering they themselves had known in their youth and fully expecting their children to be grateful for the fruits of their labours. Far from being grateful, however, their children grew up to despise and reject the world they saw around them, the world they thought their parents had created. To the young it was a grasping, greedy way of life, created by hate and war and governed by material values. So they rebelled against it; they grew their hair long, wore dirty, ragged clothes, all the things that would shock the society that they so much deplored. The natural consequences of this reaction was to return to the simple life that Jesus had led, a life in which money plays no part and all the glossy trappings of the modern world are meaningless. This is of course a gross simplification but basically that is what happened and the results can be seen very clearly both in Europe and in the United States.

'As a priest I should perhaps be expected to welcome this mass return to the bosom of the Church, but quite frankly I don't. The trouble is that it is a fad, and like any other fad it will pass. In other words it is not a meaningful return to God but rather a fashionable thing to do, and as such it does nothing to increase people's understanding of what religion is really about. There is a great revival of interest in witches, magic and the supernatural at the moment and it is this mystical element that these young people are searching for, not, unfortunately, God.

'I also think that there is a great danger of this kind of thing being an escape, a prop, in the same way that drugs are a prop, Instead of getting fixed on heroin you get fixed on Jesus. And that is certainly not what religion is about—God should be a real force in life, not an escape from life.

'The same misunderstanding is evident in the way in which the Church's involvement in the everyday world is assumed to be limited by the fact that the clergy do not live the same kind of life as other people. Because we take vows of celibacy, because therefore we have no families, and because we live in a simple way this sets us apart from everyone else. But to think in this way is to completely misunderstand the role of the clergy. As a priest, I am here to bear witness to a different kind of life, to the elements in human nature and the human condition which are not normally brought out. For instance I choose to live a life of celibacy, but many other people are celibate through no choice of their own, because circumstances have denied them sexual fulfilment. I think it is right, therefore, that

I and others like me should bear witness to that kind of life, to show that this is an area of human experience that many people are denied. This does not mean to say that I believe that priests should not be allowed to marry, on the contrary I believe very strongly that they should be given the right to choose for themselves and I'm sure that very soon they will be. But that does not in any way lessen the value of celibacy for those like myself who choose it.

'It is the same with poverty. Priests who reject material things, and more particularly nuns who take vows of poverty, are, I believe, doing something very valuable. People in affluent societies tend to forget the millions who are starving, who will never be anything but poor, and I believe it is right for a group of people to bear witness to the poverty that exists in the world.

'We realize of course that entering the priesthood or becoming a nun can never really be the same as true poverty because it always carries with it total security. Anyone who enters the Church knows that he or she will never have to worry about finding a bed for tonight or food for tomorrow. Immediate needs are always taken care of. Nevertheless I still believe that it is a good thing for human beings to choose to deny themselves many of life's luxuries, good for the human race as a whole that is, not just for the people who do it.

'Going back to the question of riches and the Church itself, I do believe that the Church should always have enough money to be able to maintain its independence from the state. No religious organization can hope to function meaningfully if it is in the pocket of the government, because it then becomes subject to political pressure and so ceases to be free. Independence is vital because I believe that Church officials, who after all occupy a privileged position in society, have a duty to speak out against oppression and moral injustice wherever they find it. The bishops in South Africa are an obvious example of the Church going against the policies of the government. This is a vital role for the clergy everywhere to undertake—after all if they fail to speak out against cruelty and oppression then what is the justification for their existence?

'I realize of course that religion itself has been the cause of much bloodshed not only in the past but even today. This is something that I can only deplore for I cannot begin to explain it or understand it any more than anyone else has done. I just hope and pray that one day people will learn to take pleasure in their differences instead of warring over them. Perhaps in practical terms that is the greatest thing that the Church has to offer, for the knowledge that all of us are equal in the eyes of God is the first important step towards peace.'

Father Michaels has certainly found his own personal peace. He radiates a rare contentment which those who are with him cannot fail to notice and which many people, both rich and poor, would no doubt envy. The same contentment is immediately apparent on the face of Sister Teresa, a young and strikingly attractive nun who lives in a convent outside London. Before becoming a nun she was a teacher with lots of boyfriends and enough money to buy pretty clothes and visit the hairdresser every week. Now she has nothing, yet she is happier than at any time in the whole of her previous life.

CHAPTER FOURTEEN

The convent

Sister Maria Teresa entered the order of Poor Child Jesus thirteen years ago when she was twenty-one years old. She would have entered earlier but her father (a non-Catholic) refused to give his consent, hoping that the daughter he loved so much would come to change her mind and find a husband instead. After all she had always been such a bright, laughing child, a keen football fan and an ardent follower of the latest fashions—it was inconceivable that she should want to be a nun! But Teresa did not change her mind, and after obtaining a teaching diploma she filled in the time until her twenty-first birthday by taking a job in a primary school. Having attained adult status she was then free to follow her vocation and, hoping fervently that her father would come to understand in the end, she took her first step into a religious life of poverty, chastity and obedience.

The outside world tends to think of nuns as demure, rather plain girls who walk with their heads bowed and have little interest in the lighter side of life. In Sister Teresa's case nothing could be further from the truth. She is a small, gay person with bright eyes and a ready laugh and when she takes off her veil (which she does frequently on her many car journeys to different parts of the country) her long, red hair flows over her shoulders. She is obviously happy and content and her active life in the convent where she teaches allows her plenty of time to visit her parents who live nearby. Her father has finally come to terms with the fact that his favourite daughter has given herself to God, and he is even proud of it. After all she does still support Tottenham Hotspurs so perhaps she has not changed as much as he had feared.

But of course Teresa has changed. Thirteen years of living with women, of wearing the same black dress and veil every day of her life, and of having nothing to call her own, all these things have made her a very different person from the successful head teacher she would undoubtedly have become had she pursued an independent career outside the convent. Her fresh, unmade-up face bears none of the signs of stress, none of the furrows of hardship and experience that come from living in a physical, competitive world. And yet Teresa herself freely admits that though she herself owns nothing and strives for nothing in a material sense she has still not lost the feeling of enjoyment that these things can bring. She may have nothing that belongs to her personally but she still has access to a great many things that other people only dream of. In her own eyes she is not poor at all.

'I believe that we have given the world a wrong concept of the meaning of the vow of poverty. The word itself is even misleading because real poverty—the condition in which the necessities of life are lacking—is an international evil which we want to eliminate. In our sense of the word poverty is simply part of the process of giving oneself to God. After all it is just not possible to devote oneself to spiritual fulfilment if one is constantly concerned about paying the next instalment on the car or buying a new dress for a cocktail party. I chose religious poverty because I wanted to put my love of God at the disposal of others and in order to do this I had to be freed from pursuing material ends for myself.

'But that does not mean to say that material possessions are unhealthy and I myself am very critical of the Church for suggesting, as it has done for some time, that this is the case. We do not proclaim loudly enough the joy of life, the gifts of creation that are all around us to be enjoyed, not spurned as evil.

'I am well aware that we as a community own very much more than many lay people. We have a car, each of us has a small but adequate room of our own, we have books, bright furniture, plenty to eat and drink and the security of a permanent home. I am sure that there must be people who feel that this is not poverty, that we are being hypocritical in having so much and enjoying so much.

'I can only say, in answer to that, that poverty for us is not a sentimental, devotional copying of Christ's earthly life, nor is it a renunciation of money for money's sake because it corrupts. Rather it is a willingness to give oneself, to cease holding on to things and to put oneself at the service of others. To give you a practical example —we have a car, a Renault, which I love driving and which I perhaps drive more than most of the other Sisters. But I know that if I want to go somewhere for the week-end and someone else needs the car for another reason then I cannot have it. Often this is hard to accept because I admit that, rightly or wrongly, one does begin to feel a certain possessiveness about the things one enjoys using. And in a way it is harder to have them and have no rights over them than it is not to have them at all. Even my time is not my own, for if I set aside an hour to do some private studying and someone asks me to do something then I will leave my studying and go and do it.

'I do think that it is much harder for women not to be possessive about things than it is for men. Women tend to identify more with the objects around them, with nice china, home furnishings and so on, and of course they find it hard to look at pretty clothes in the shop windows and know that they cannot have them. Even now I sometimes see something I particularly like and think how lovely it would be to be able to wear it. Of course I know I can't, not even when I go home to stay with my parents; I must still wear my black dress and veil.

'I think that being in an active order where you are constantly coming face to face with the things that you have formally rejected is in many ways a harder test of your strength than being in an enclosed order where you have little or no contact with the outside world. We have complete freedom to go to the theatre, cinema, watch television, read and see what we please. Of course we have to ask for the money to go anywhere because our teaching salary goes straight into the convent's bank account, but, providing that one is not going out every night and leaving everyone else to do all the work, there is usually no problem in getting the money one needs. In some cases this freedom has simply proved too much for people and certainly since I have been here several nuns have been unable to resist the temptations that they saw around them and have left to go back to their previous life. It is hard to know how far one should go in this respect. Some orders even believe that nuns should go further still and wear ordinary dress (and indeed they do in some cases) but I think that this makes them painfully vulnerable both physically and emotionally. A nun's habit does at least offer some protection which to my mind is absolutely essential. After all, in spite of our faith, we are still human beings underneath.'

Certainly few people recognize the hardship of belonging to an active religious order in which one is constantly confronted with the things one has given up. All too often it is considered a soft option, a compromise undertaken by those who are too faint-hearted to go the whole way and undertake a total religious commitment. But whether one believes it is too soft or too hard, one fact remains indisputable and that is that for more than four years now the order of Poor Child Jesus has received no applications for entry in nine out of the thirteen countries in which it exists. The nine countries in question are all part of the affluent European block, while the remaining four (which have more than their fill of applicants) are all economically poor.

But if the active religious orders seem to be finding it hard to attract young women in affluent societies, the lesser known and seldom seen enclosed orders are having no trouble at all. One such order is the Poor Clares, a community of silent, brown-robed nuns who walk barefoot on bare boards and whose only contact with the outside world is a telephone and a weekly Catholic newspaper, the *Tablet*. These closely veiled women take four solemn vows—poverty, chastity, obedience and enclosure—and they emerge from the confines of their convent only in cases of dire necessity such as ill health.

There are twenty Poor Clare convents in the British Isles, most of them known only to the local inhabitants and members of the clergy. These settlements are really poor, and their vow of poverty has a completely different meaning from that of the active orders who still teach, nurse and work in the outside world. A Poor Clare earns no money, possesses nothing, not even her patched brown habit or the photograph of her parents which she keeps in her room (these are considered to be communal property) and lives largely on providence. She sleeps on a horsehair mattress, eats no meat and little else, and enjoys none of the conveniences of modern living such as hot water every night and central heating in the winter. A wooden grille separates her from her family and friends who are allowed to visit her three times a year and, apart from talking with her visitors, a Poor Clare maintains a strict rule of silence at all times. The only other exceptions are emergencies and so-called 'recreation' which is held on four days each week and lasts for three-quarters of an hour. This means that a nun must obtain permission from the Mother Abbess to discuss with another nun a particular problem she may have, and it means too that when she does speak a Poor Clare who has been enclosed for some time tends to have a very hushed tone of voice. And yet, in spite of what appears to an outsider to be an extremely harsh and deprived way of life, the Poor Clares seem remarkably content. They laugh more easily than many a person who lives in the lap of luxury, and, though the older ones tend to be somewhat naïve, all of them, both young and old, hanker after surprisingly little that the world has to offer.

Mother Cecilia is the Abbess of a Poor Clare convent tucked away in a small country lane in the Midlands. She is a small, gentle woman with clear grey eyes and a kindly, open face and she has been inside this enclosure for over thirty years. Because of her position at the head of the community, however, Mother Cecilia has had more contact with the outside world than most of the thirty or so other nuns who live here. She speaks in little more than a whisper but her thoughts are lucid and she is clearly deeply convinced that, in spite of all the wonders of the twentieth century, life today bears little comparison with life in this thirteenth-century monastic order.

'I entered the convent in 1939 when I was twenty-two years old. I was a trained teacher at the time but I chose to come here rather than go into a teaching order because I wanted total commitment. An active religious life means that you are still involved in the system of money-making, even if you are not quite as tied as people in the outside world. I find it strange that we should be looked upon as restricted by people who consider themselves to be free. How can they be free when they are worrying about buying a new car, getting a better job, keeping up with the latest fashions and keeping ahead of the next-door neighbour? The more money you have the more tied you become and the less able you are to reach beyond material things to higher and deeper levels of experience. Certainly the faces I see on the rare occasions when I leave this convent are not happy faces. Everyone seems to be rushing somewhere, to be distracted, worried, engrossed in some problem or other. There is so little love in the world; it seems to me that people have no time for love any more.

'From what I hear, though, it does seem that some young people are at last moving away from the outward signs of affluence. When I came into this convent it was very much the thing to look smart and well-groomed; now I believe that people are buying clothes that look old, dirty and even frayed and that smartness is no longer desirable. If this is so then I am sure it is a good thing, for it shows an understanding of the fact that it is the person that matters and not how he or she may happen to look.

'As an ex-teacher I feel that the system of education is desperately at fault in perpetuating the evils or affluence.

Children are not educated to live a full and meaningful life but to earn a good living and make money. They do not even have time to think for themselves, they go from this exam to that exam, constantly being crammed full of facts. By the time they are able to stop and evaluate things it is often too late. They have been brainwashed to the point where they can no longer think of life in other than material terms. But having a good job and earning lots of money is not what life is about, nor is learning a whole stream of facts and figures. None of these things make for happiness and they certainly do not teach one to cope with life's problems.

'Personally I would be quite horrified at the prospect of having a great deal of money. Wealth brings with it an enormous burden of responsibility, for there is so much poverty and misery in the world that it would be impossible to know how best to put it to good use. Those who ignore the pain and suffering and simply pursue their own selfish ends must surely find it hard to sleep easily in their beds at night.

'But if it is difficult to know how to handle money wisely it is certainly no easy thing to give up everything as we do, and to do without the pleasures that one has come to love and enjoy. But then the sacrifice is valuable precisely because it is hard—if it were easy then there would be little point—and of course it brings its own, very much higher rewards in the end.

'Just what we miss of the outside world varies very much with each individual. Personally the things that I miss most are a good play and a long, brisk walk on a summer's day. I know that some of the other Sisters find it hard to do without newspapers and radio, and a few of the younger ones pine for pretty clothes and the car they used to drive.

But these things pass and when they do one finds how much beauty there is in simple things. After all, those who have too much of the so-called good things of life eventually become bored with their expensive caviar and champagne while we on the other hand find increasing pleasure in something as modest as a lettuce sandwich eaten outside in the sunshine.

'This is why I so regret the passing of primitive societies. Their way of life is far superior to that of the zealous missionaries who come along to hustle them into the twentieth century. It is such a mistake to think that progress is always desirable for its own sake and certainly as far as the primitives are concerned I am sure they have far more to lose than they have to gain.

'I should perhaps make clear just what we feel to be the relevance of our way of life because I know that there are those who accuse us of being parasites, living on charity and contributing nothing. Well we are not of course idle, we make pottery and embroidery, do printing and so on, though these things are done mainly to keep the Sisters occupied and the proceeds provide barely a quarter of our financial needs. The rest is provided by providence, and if it so happens that we have no money for bread then we do not eat. This is part of our vow of poverty, living at risk with a minimum of security.

'But this is not what our life here is really about. An enclosed order of this kind is like the heart in the body of the world. The heart is not seen and yet it is vital to the functioning of the whole, and in the same way we who live and pray for the world remain apart from it. We know that we cannot carry on without outside help but then those on the outside would be unable to carry on without our prayers.

'It takes a very special kind of girl to live an enclosed life and about half those who enter every year in the belief that they have been called by God leave before taking their final vows. Many of course come for the wrong reasons, because they want to escape from life, because they want to forget an unhappy love affair or because they are insecure in some other way. But these people never stay because if they are unable to live with themselves in the outside world they will be even more unable to live with themselves in an enclosed convent. Here you have no choice but to come face to face with yourself, to know yourself, because there is nothing to keep your mind off seeing yourself as you really are. In a convent there is no career to be involved in, no colleagues, husband or children to distract your attention, no urgent engagements to be met. This is the hardest part of living an enclosed life and those who say glibly that our way is simply an escape should stop and consider how much of their own lives is nothing but a cloak for the reality underneath. The beautiful house, fast car, loud laughter and sparkling dresses are all too often a cover for unhappy, inadequate people. Of course I realize that it takes strength to cope with the lure of material things and to handle them in the right way. Those who have no faith are particularly easy prey to earthly temptations, but you know it is so easy to do without the things that are now generally thought of as necessities. It is such a mistake to think that possessions give you freedom; on the contrary the more you have the less liberated you become. I think it is this that grieves me more than anything about the world today, for people are so terribly preoccupied with material things that they can no longer see what life is really about.'